MIRÓ

Miró

BY GASTON DIEHL

CROWN PUBLISHERS, INC. - NEW YORK

Title page: SELF-PORTRAIT I, 1937-38
Pencil and oil, 57½" x 38¹/₈"
Private Collection, New Canaan, Conn.

Photographs: Henry B. Beville, Alexandria Va. - Paul Katz, New York - Bob Mates, New York - Otto Nelson, New York - Eric Pollitzer, New York - Joseph Szaszfai, New Haven, Conn. - Alfred J. Wyatt, Philadelphia

ISBN 0-517-516713

LIBRARY OF CONGRESS CATALOG CARD NUMBER: 73-84255

ALL REPRODUCTION RIGHTS TO THE PHOTOGRAPHS BY A.D.A.G.P., PARIS

PRINTED IN ITALY - © 1974 BY PALLAS SCRIPT AGENCY S. A. NAEFELS, SUISSE

THE VILLAGE, PRADES, 1917. Oil, 26¹/₈" x 29"
Collection: The Solomon R. Guggenheim Museum, New York

Many unfortunate careers in the arts have led to a belief that in our age artistic genius must subsist almost exclusively on sufferings endured and misfortunes encountered, and that its only path was scandal, rejection by society, rebellion, or death.

Thus when we encounter a life that is visibly happy and uneventful, we are somewhat hesitant to talk about a success of such exceptional nature, and we feel obliged to supply suitable explanations.

One example is the case of Joan Miró. Throughout his life success has been, and continues to be, his constant companion. No one would dream of challenging or begrudging him this success, yet we feel it should be explained and justified because it is so different from that of other artists. Such unvarying good fortune, and the rapid achievement of such brilliant results, is a sufficiently rare phenomenon to merit attention and close examination.

While Miró seems to have benefited at a relatively early age from good fortune of an extremely rare sort, he owes his success first of all to himself, his quiet persistence, and his dogged labor, which enabled him to overcome his early difficulties, and to his determination to rise above the customary formulas, even the most modern ones. He did not hesitate to use these, however, in order to rediscover the forces of instinct as well as to reestablish a relationship with the earliest traditions surviving through the millennia.

It is this very special procedure, which he used with an integrity and a lucidity unequaled by any other artist, that immediately elevates him to the ranks of the leading spirits of our age. His is the role of the pioneer, the herald of a new concept that was quickly to gain ground: the idea of the equality of races and civilizations. His inventive pictography with its quasi-magical signs and his symbolism derived from the most remote aspects of the heritage of the popular arts have become a common living language accessible to all people. His work possesses to a high degree a tendency toward the universal, which greatly helped to increase its triumphant spread throughout the world.

As J. J. Sweeney predicted very early in Miró's career, the extremely daring and deliberate boldness of his efforts have won for him one of the leading positions in contemporary art, unchallenged by any comer. By his demand for absolute liberty, his many plastic and poetic discoveries, his exceptional feeling for matter, and his recourse to a supreme simplicity, he has demonstrated an incomparable openness and accessibility that subsequently served as an encouragement and an example to numerous artists, and undoubtedly to the creators of the cartoon and the comic strip as well. Without ever having sought or desired to do so, he anticipated, victoriously initiated, and often became thoroughly involved in the principal movements that developed in the past quarter of a century in Spain, France, the United States, Japan, and many other countries. Inevitably, then, he is to a certain extent regarded as the spiritual father of most of the leaders of the present avant-garde, and his authority is proportionately broadened and reinforced.

Many reasons militate in favor of the long-acknowledged confirmation of Miró's art in its various aspects. The tributes paid to him with increasing frequency at the Galerie and Fondation Maeght, and particularly on the international level in Berne and Basel (1949), Germany (1954), Brussels and Amsterdam (1956), New York and Los Angeles (1959), Paris (1962), London and Zurich (1964), Tokyo and Kyoto (1966), at the Fondation Maeght and in Barcelona (1968), Munich (1969), Stockholm (1972), and again and with unparalleled amplitude in Paris in 1974, all attest to the widening scope of his power.

However, this unanimity concerning the unquestionable merit of his contribution was not won without struggle and difficulties. We must first examine the stages of his career before going on to consider the basic character of this creative genius, who has succeeded in leaving his imprint on a great variety of techniques, with a baffling simplicity of means and a strength of intensity that cannot be equaled.

THE SPELL OF THE LAND

None of Miró's biographers — and they are legion — has failed to stress his continuing close relationship with the place of his birth and childhood. The artist himself has frequently spoken of the extreme importance he attaches to his native land — to Barcelona, Montroig, Majorca. Moreover, he has always maintained a residence there, and his sojourns in the region have become increasingly frequent.

It is essential to give first consideration to this earliest influence and not to belittle its importance. Since I feel that in the cases of both Picasso and Miró this Spanish (more specifically Catalan, in the case of Miró) influence was the predominant and most important factor, I subscribe all the more willingly to this principle.

What traveler has not fallen under the spell of this region of Spain? I myself became acquainted with it between 1932 and 1936, when it was still wild and off the beaten tourist track. Who at that time could have resisted the allure of the Costa Brava, with its deserted beaches inhabited only by fishing boats, vividly colored and with eyes painted on them to ward off evil, its wild, rocky headlands and steep slopes, its coves with their blue waters that remained transparent to the very bottom, its luxuriant foliage, its sky of unparalleled limpidity, and its brilliant nocturnal spectacles? Who could have failed to be impressed by the proud nobility, vivacious manner, and individualism of an entire race at that time under the spell of the voice of Campanys, the diversity of a craft tradition that had remained almost intact, the impudent eroticism flaunted in the Barrio Chino, and still more by the spectacle, on holidays, of the main square of Barcelona completely overrun and seething with the surges of an immense crowd swaying and twirling to the happy strains of the sardana? Who could have forgotten the miniatures of the Apocalypse of San Sever, the frescoes of San Clemente and Santa Maria de Tahull, and the Apocalypse tapestry in the Cathedral of Gerona, which visibly influenced Miró when he was formulating his stylistic objectives and formal repertoire?

Miró is very much a member of this dynamic and hardworking race, which possesses a sense of organization and has its feet on the ground but is also endowed with imagination, motivated by the desire for independence and escape, and blessed with innate ability and dexterity, a craftsman's sensitivity to material, and an astonishing faculty of observation and adaptation. As a true Catalan, Miró demonstrates simplicity of reception and smiling affability, complemented or compensated for by a discreet reserve, a natural uncommunicativeness and secrecy, and a tendency to solemnity and spirituality. In self-defense he continually resorts to ingenuousness, whimsy, and humor, which poorly conceal a feverish anxiety and a fundamental anguish, found in every Spaniard, before the omnipresent thought of the twin poles of existence: sex and death. Miró does not hesitate to reexamine continually the bases of existence.

It must be remembered that he spent the first 26 years of his life confined in this environment because of the winding down of the First World War. But he did not permit himself to be deluded or restricted by his affection for it, which was so great that he returned there every summer (except during the period 1936 - 1940). His native land stimulated him; he drew his sustenance from the ocean breeze that is the charm of Barcelona; the Art Nouveau allure of the Pasaje del Credito, where he was born on April 20, 1893; the « Aquarium, » as his father's watch and jewelry shop was called, which name tempted him to associate water and fire with a desire for strict organization; the swaying of the palms against the sky; the ubiquitous murmur of the fountains in the patios and public squares; and the lyrical ardor of the works of Gaudi, which he saw being constructed in the Parc Güell and at the Church of the Holy Family.

We should like to believe, since he has told us, that his « need for order and tranquillity » took pleasure in contemplating the classical Roman arches of Tarragona. But his youthful gaze did not linger long on the urban aspect of his country. He early preferred nature and rural scenes, as is proved by the extremely detailed, diligent drawings he made, with unusual precocity, between the ages of 8 and 13, before he had any artistic instruction. In his carefully preserved pictures on pieces of paper and in notebooks, he sometimes makes a detailed examination of a flower or a fish, with attention worthy of any adult; in others, he profits by his sojourn in the country, with his paternal grandparents in Cornudella or his maternal grandparents on Majorca. His father's father was a blacksmith, and, like any child, Miró took an enthusiastic interest in blacksmith work and the making of irons for branding livestock. For the time being, he was satisfied to sketch with sobriety and an astonishing strength the austere composition of the landscape and the church surrounded by the houses of his village or the neighboring villages of Ciurana and Prades, themes that he was to repeat several years later in his painting. The recollection of his travels to the home of his mother's father, a cabinetmaker and businessman who died at an early age was material for his daydreams before the mill on Majorca, which he carefully sketched. After 1910, in Montroig, where his parents had purchased a farm, he plunged more ardently into peasant life.

Wherever he went, he was imbued with the environment and distilled from it every element that was later to reappear in his memories of his childhood, his childish emotions and surprises: the teeming diversity of nature, the skill of the craftsman, and the wealth of popular art, particularly in Majorca, where the dual Eastern and esoteric heritage that was to influence him so profoundly had been maintained and preserved through the ages.

He also reveals his joy at finding himself far from Barcelona, where his vexations and difficulties were steadily increasing. As he told Jacques Dupin, his most faithful biographer, he was not a brilliant success in the little school in the Calle Regomir, where he began his studies at the age of seven. He felt humiliated by his classmates, and he was bored with school, except in the elective drawing courses, which he attended religiously. He also had to face increasing incomprehension on the part of his father, who nevertheless permitted him to register in 1907 at both the Business School and the « La Llotja » School of Fine Arts, where three years later he experienced the same failure, due in this case to the academic instruction imparted. He is nevertheless grateful to his teachers, Modesto

8

NORTH-SOUTH, 1917
Oil, 24^1/$_8$" x 27^5/$_8$"
Collection: Galerie Maeght, Paris

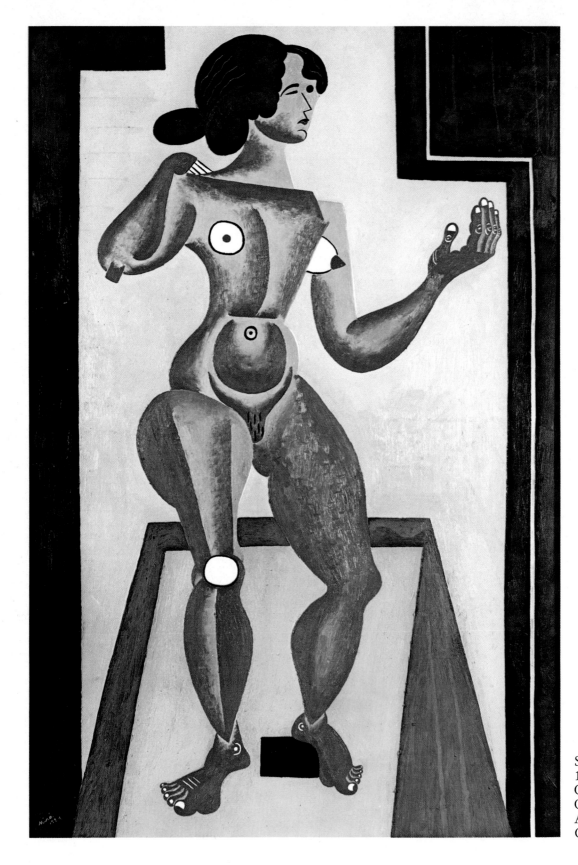

STANDING NUDE,
1921
Oil, 51¹/₈" x 35¹/
Collection:
Alsdorf Foundation
Chicago, Ill.

Nude with Mirror, 1919. Oil, 44¹/₈″ x 40¹/₈″
Collection: Kunstsammlung Nordrhein-Westfalen, Düsseldorf

THE VILLAGE OF MONTROIG, 1919. Oil, 28³/₄" x 24"
Collection: Sra. Miró de Fernandez, Palma de Majorca

Urgell and José Pasco, who on occasion gave him helpful advice. Finally, having abandoned all hope of bringing his artistic vocation to fruition, at the age of 17 and at his father's wish he became a bookkeeper for Dalmau & Oliveras, a large drugstore. Two years later, his health undermined by the absurdity of this existence, and preyed upon by a secret rebellion, he suffered a nervous depression complicated by an attack of typhoid fever. In a greatly weakened condition he left to convalesce at Montroig, where he sketched constantly while recovering his health.

In 1912 his family finally permitted him to follow his wishes and register at a private art school that had been established a short time previously by Francisco Galí. Until 1915 Galí was to encourage and direct his efforts to the best of his ability, developing his sense of form by ingenious tactile exercises and orienting him toward sure appreciation of modern art, ranging from Van Gogh to the Cubists. His fellow pupils became his first friends; they included Manuel Grau, the future specialist in Catalan frescoes, and E. C. Ricart, with whom he shared a studio in 1915 in the calle Baja de San Pedro. During this period he also frequented the San Lluc Art Club, which was installed in a predestined location: the building that had previously housed the famous « Quatro Gatos » Cabaret, the meeting place of young Picasso and his friends. Here, until 1918, Miró was able to draw from life, participate in lively discussions, and above all establish decisive relationships with Joan Prats, who remained his closest friend until his death, Llorens Artigas, with whom Miró was to create his ceramic works, J. F. Rafols, Sebastia Gasch, who later wrote articles and recollections about him, Maria Espinal, Josep Obiols, and others.

Although he continued to seek frequent refuge and inspiration from his solitary sojourns in the country at Montroig, Cornudella, and their surroundings (whence he wrote impassioned letters to his friends), Miró had nevertheless made his peace with his native city, where he now felt completely at ease. In the absence of his family and his sister, who gave him scant assistance, he found in Barcelona a favorable atmosphere and the assurance of his comrades' support.

As a consequence of the war, relationships between Barcelona and France became much closer, and possibilities for exchanges increased greatly. In particular, the gallery managed by Joseph Dalmau (who as early as 1912 had committed his resources in support of Picasso, Léger, and Marcel Duchamp) regularly showed the Fauves' and Cubists' works, and became a center of information where Catalan intellectuals met each evening and welcomed French painters and poets passing through the city. Thus Miró had an opportunity to meet the critic Maurice Raynal (who later wrote an introduction for his Paris exhibition) and Francis Picabia, just back from New York, who was sometimes accompanied by Marie Laurencin, at other times by Max Jacob. He became familiar with the avant-garde magazines *Les Soirées de Paris* and *Nord-Sud*, as is evident from his paintings, and already enjoyed the poetry of Apollinaire, Reverdy, P. A. Birot, and other poets whom Junoy was then making great efforts to translate. Emboldened by this propitious atmosphere and strengthened in his resolutions, he succeeded in obtaining from Dalmau the promise of an exhibition as soon as he had assembled a sufficient number of paintings, which was done, with that zeal and meticulousness we can guess, by February of 1918. It was high time, and the event was of major importance in Miró's life, for now, at the age of 25, he had at any price to take revenge on destiny and assert his existence to himself and even more to his family and his countrymen.

While his drawings very quickly grew lighter, more animated, and more refined, his painting (begun between 1914 and 1915) continued to be heavy, dark, hesitant, and trapped in materiality. But his obstinate efforts, based on selected examples and models undoubtedly available to him, led him after 1917 to more valid solutions. Still lifes and landscapes, at first obviously inspired by Cézanne and Matisse, also make use of the traditional expressionist content, which served Miró as his authority to better externalize his temperament and to introduce more spirit and brilliance into his canvases. Thus, in several views of *The Church of Ciurana, A Street in Prades,* and particularly in *North-South* with its simultaneous concentric circles, he succeeded in achieving a freer, rhythmic, colored structure. In *The Balcony in the Baja San Pedro* he also experimented with the Cubist lesson, which he took as his authority for the inclusion in several paintings (*Path in Ciurana, The Village of Prades*) of a decorative, medieval type of stylization consisting of broken lines and parallel chevrons in vivid alternating colors, reminiscent of the furrows in a field.

In the fervor of his momentum he tackled the human figure for the first time in 1917. With a conspiratorial and unself-conscious nod to Cézanne (in *Women Playing Cards* and *La Maria*), between 1917 and 1919 he painted a series of portraits that are direct descendants of Van Gogh's works, but are deflected along an unexpected and divergent path by the violence of the contours, contrasts, and harmonies, and by the persistent presence of parallel, almost proto-kinetic bands and awkward distortions. In the most typical of these portraits, that of the painter E. C. Ricart, whose studio Miró shared, and who also used his friends as models, he disconcertingly contrasts the extraordinary subtlety of a Japanese silk, copied with a high degree of vigor and detail, with coarseness of outline and feature and a fauvist play of colors.

It is not surprising that this exhibition, with its frequently inconsistent aspects and impulses, aroused little enthusiasm on the part of visitors to the Dalmau Gallery and met with more irony than esteem. It must nevertheless be acknowledged that such a beginning was very promising, since in barely three years of artistic labor Miró had been able to make use, with great discernment, of the contemporary movements available to him, from Expressionism to Cubism by way of Fauvism, and to isolate a language of his age that was already close to the level of the language being used by Delaunay, Le Fauconnier, Gondouin, Maria Blanchard, and other artists.

Undiscouraged, he continued his line of attack and completed two paintings that are both significant and revelatory of his dilemma. By virtue of its subject, the painting entitled *Standing Nude,* with its abundantly flower-patterned wall hanging and rug, appears to be a final tribute to Matisse, but a tribute rendered paradoxical by the aggressive schematism and in the size of the body, which is treated like a Negro statue. The other painting, *Still Life with Coffee Mill,* follows a strict analytical constructivism, humorously complemented by a collage in the form of a ticket from New York, perhaps given to him by Picabia. However, as was his habit he felt the need to retire to Montroig for a rather long period, in order to escape the blandishments of fashion and his friends and search his soul more deeply.

In the rural solitude he rediscovered certain sensations of his childhood, and began an important reconversion that he describes with great relevance in a frequently quoted letter to Rafols: « When I set to work on a landscape, I begin by loving it, with that love which is the child of slow understanding. Slow understanding of the great wealth of nuances — a concentrated wealth — provided by the sun. Happiness of attaining understanding of a blade of grass in the landscape — Why should we disdain it? — this blade of grass that is as beautiful as a tree or a mountain. No one, with the exception of the Primitives and the Japanese, had really made a close examination of this divine object. We seek out and paint only the large masses of the trees and mountains, without listening to the music that emanates from the tiny flowers, the blades of grass, and the little stones in the ravine. »

In this state of amorous ecstasy just described, and which is in truth close to the spirit of the Primitives and the Japanese, he painted from nature a remarkable series of landscapes — *House with Palm Tree, Kitchen Garden with Donkey,* and *The Rut,* among others — whose strange charm springs from their carefully measured blend of poetry and simplicity. Noticeable changes have taken place, revealing a visible pleasure in the work: a simplified and carefully thought-out arrangement, an evolution toward a two-dimensional space, use of flat color areas and a soft, varied chromatic scale, and above all minute attention paid to the details of plants, branches, walls, and clouds, as in old Eastern miniatures. He was so pleased with these landscapes that he reserved them for a new group, the « *Agrupación Courbet,* » founded by Artigas, who showed them the following year at the Municipal Exhibition. During the winter in Barcelona he painted portraits, including his own, in a similar aesthetic style. This *Self Portrait,* which thanks to its affected mannerism, authoritative elimination of the superfluous, curvilinear rhythms, and quiet hierarchism seems to have come straight out of a Romanesque fresco, belongs in fact to the same current termed « detailist » by Rafols and « poetically realist » by Dupin. In any event its delightful originality enchanted Picasso, who soon purchased it, undoubtedly to help his young compatriot subsist in Paris, and kept it for good.

Between March and June of 1919 Miró succeeded, although not without difficulty, in fulfilling a dream he and his friends had long cherished, but which had been delayed by the postwar adjustment period and the influenza epidemic: a trip to the French capital to visit museums and galleries and to establish contacts with a view to settling in Paris later. His own character and his precarious financial resources obliged him to take certain precautions before setting out on such an adventure.

Elated and overwhelmed by this trip despite its brevity, upon his return to Barcelona he settled down to work, his enthusiasm increased by an agreement made with

Dalmau that assured him of a small sum of money and an exhibition in Paris in return for his recent output, as he immediately reported to Ricart. In the handful of works that he now painted, he seems to have wanted to say farewell to his most recent stage of development. Particularly in *The Church and Village of Montroig,* and in *Seated Nude* (painted in Barcelona and perhaps based on some Japanese print), he drew together at will difficulties of detailed rendering, rigorous drawing, and a skillful chromatic organization directed at monumentality, suddenly combined (in the latter painting) with attempts at Cubist schematization. This experiment is more elaborate and more successful in *Vines and Olive Trees in Montroig,* in which carefully observed details and colored groupings suggesting collages or intersecting planes freely alternate, the result being a supremely evocative, sumptuous celebration of his favorite scenes that links the past and the future. By the joyous, carefully laid out network of rows of furrows, repetitive silhouettes of plants, trees, and mountain peaks, complemented by overlays of color and decorative whimsies, and by the daring invention of genuine plastic signs of a visible symbolism, he masterfully anticipates the future before him.

At the time, his stay in Paris during the winter of 1919 and the spring of 1920 produced no results; lacking a studio and favorable surroundings, he was unable to work there. He became slightly acquainted with Reverdy and Tzara, and attended the Dada manifestation and festival with them. The influence of this movement, however, did not penetrate his work until later.

The works he painted during the summer of 1920 in Montroig have more resemblance to an inventory of the resources and possibilities of a Cubism reexamined in the light of « The New Spirit, » ranging from Juan Gris to Ozenfant, and still more to a personal restatement of the problems of form and color in space. Here again, in *Spanish Card Game, The Horse, Pipe and Red Flower,* and *Still Life with Rabbit,* we are witnessing a rather grandiloquent, baroque ceremony prior to departure, and an attempt to establish an extremely detailed catalog of the beloved and admired world that was already becoming part of the world of childhood, before he withdrew from it and saw it change and disappear. For, as he told Ricart, and as Dupin mentions, he was determined henceforth to put Paris before Barcelona, in order to avoid falling into somnolence and mummification. He already intended to « become an international Catalan. »

Despite the rigors of a second Paris winter (that of 1920, which lasted until the end of May 1921), endured with difficulty because of the lack of money, his working and living conditions were improving, and his plans were gradually taking shape. He had a studio, loaned to him by Gargallo, in the rue Blomet, and here, with Masson and thanks to Max Jacob, he met a group of people to whom he become increasingly close, and which included Robert Desnos, Michel Leiris, Georges Limbour, and others. The exhibition promised by Dalmau opened on April 29 at the Galerie La Licorne in the rue la Boétie, with a perspicacious preface by Raynal, who must have introduced him to Cubist circles. The hoped-for commercial success did not materialize, but this exhibition to a certain extent called attention to him and brought him some consideration. To encourage him, before his departure from

THE FARM, 1921-22
Oil, 48¹/₄" x 55¹/₄". Private collection

THE EAR OF GRAIN, 1922-23
Oil, 14⁷/₈" x 18¹/₈".
Collection: Museum of Modern Art, New York

18

The Tilled Field, 1923-24
Oil, 26" x 37".
Collection: The Solomon R. Guggenheim Museum, New York

20

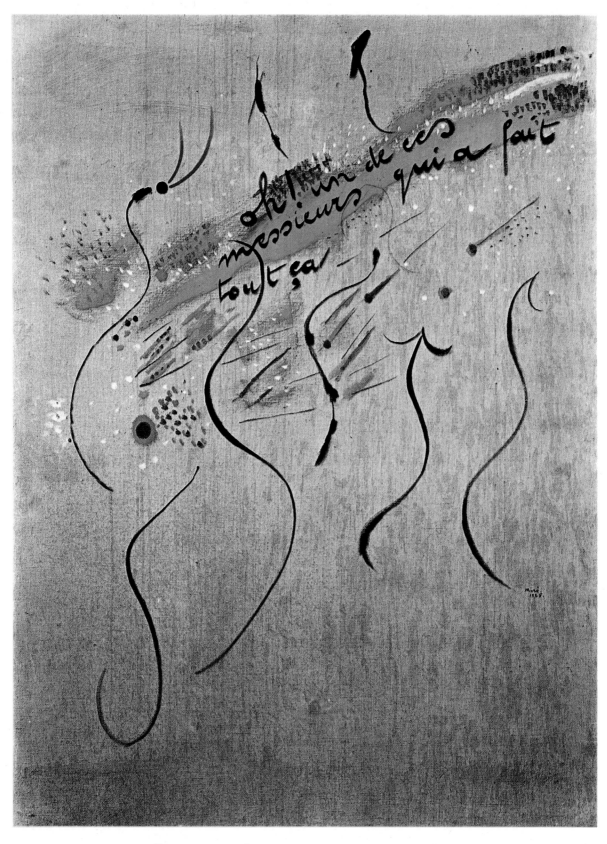

« Oh! un de ces Messieurs qui a fait tout ça » 1925
Picture-Poem, Oil, 51¹/₈" x 37³/₈". Collection: Galerie Maeght, Paris

22

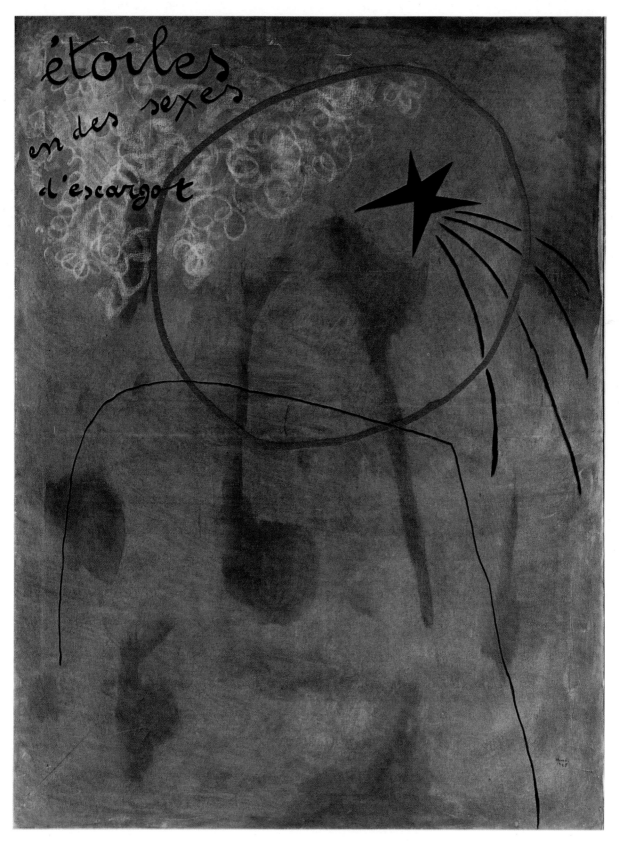

« Etoiles en des sexes d'escargot », 1925
Picture-Poem, Oil, 51¹/₈" x 38¹/₈". Collection: Kunstsammlung Nordrhein-Westfalen, Düsseldorf

Person Throwing a Stone at a Bird, 1926
Oil, 29" x 36¼"
Collection: Museum of Modern Art, New York

The Statue, 1925
Oil, 31½" x 25⅝" ▷
Collection: Marcel Mabille, Bruxelles

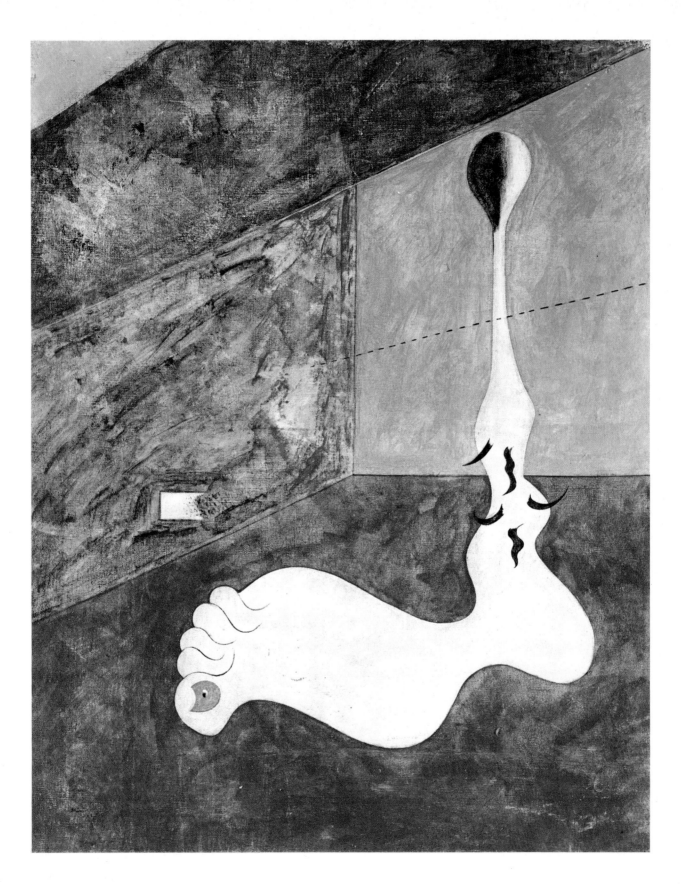

Paris, Picasso purchased from him *Portrait of a Spanish Dancer,* which Miró had just completed and which reveals a very pronounced hieratic, refined realism.

Hardly had Miró returned to Montroig when he undertook, with increased eagerness and in an appropriate format, the preparation of a grandiose synthesis of all his efforts: *The Farm,* in which he wished to achieve the final apotheosis of this period. He was obliged to take the large canvas to his studio in the rue Blomet, where he finished it several months later.

All the folklore experienced during his childhood has its place in this moving farewell in which the real is already transposed into a dream, in this marriage between heaven and earth, in this seductive, pagan festival which he has patiently reconstructed. Each mineral, vegetable, animal, and human element is inventoried, isolated, and detached in order to be magnified, plunged back into brilliant light and into the innocence of memory, positioned in a suitable space, and assembled to size. Thus by an infallible orchestration of the colored planes with their soft modulations, all the elements are harmoniously organized and develop marvelously in a coherent, dense, rhythmic sculptural ensemble in which the smallest symbol acquires a power of incantation, becomes weighted with a poetic resonance, and is transformed into a living symbol, which the viewer may analyze at will and interpret personally. Although rightfully considered by its author as one of the high points of his output, the painting unfortunately did not immediately find a buyer. It was purchased several years later by Ernest Hemingway, acting on the advice of the poet Evan Shipman.

While he persevered in this spirit of synthesis, we can nevertheless feel that he was tense, disturbed, perhaps ill at ease about his apparent undue closeness to Ozenfant and Léger. He parodies himself in *Table with Glove, Standing Nude,* and, not without a humor that holds promise for the future, in *Spanish Dancer.*

In the following year (1922/1923), without studio or permanent lodging in Paris, and laboring under severe difficulties, we find him still more preoccupied and (in *The Carbide Lamp* and *Ear of Wheat*) anxious to discover the evil spell that emanates, as in Picabia's pictures, from objects detached from their context, and whose very presence becomes aggressive and strange. Fortunately he regained his self-possesson, stimulated, I believe, by the example of Picasso, and this first and extremely decisive portion of his life ends on a note of beauty. In *The Farmer's Wife* he summarizes his rural impressions, treating them ironically, like an *image d'Epinal* or, more precisely, like monumental *santons,* the gaily colored clay figurines that populate the Provençal Nativity crèche. For the last time he sums up his previous experiences by rejecting the contemporary movements he had just investigated. On the other side of the frontier, thanks to his resolute simplifications of both forms and colors, his fractionations and geometric schematizations bordering on abstraction, and his distortions and enlargements, he was already opening the door, with magnificent daring, to plastic metaphors and the imaginary.

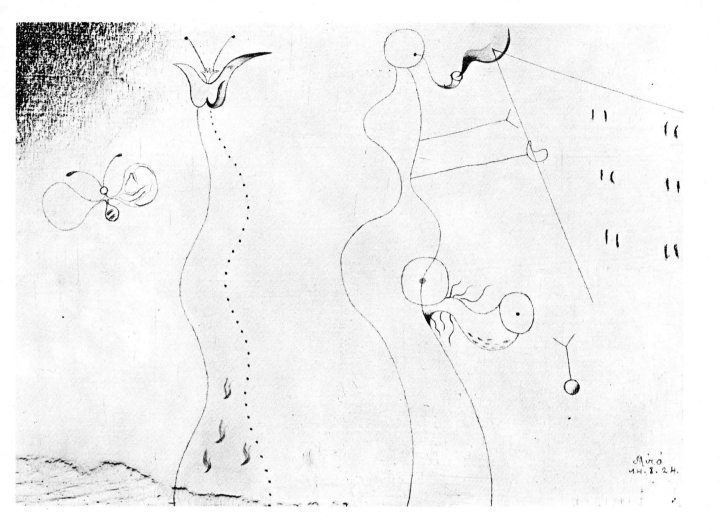

Composition, 1924. Pencil
Collection: Wadsworth Atheneum, Hartford, Conn.

MATERNITY, 1924.
Oil, 35⁷/₈" x 29¹/₈" Collection: Sir Roland Penrose, London

THE SOMMERSAULT, 1924. Oil, charcoal and tempera, 36¼" x 28¾"
Collection: Yale University Art Gallery, New Haven, Conn.

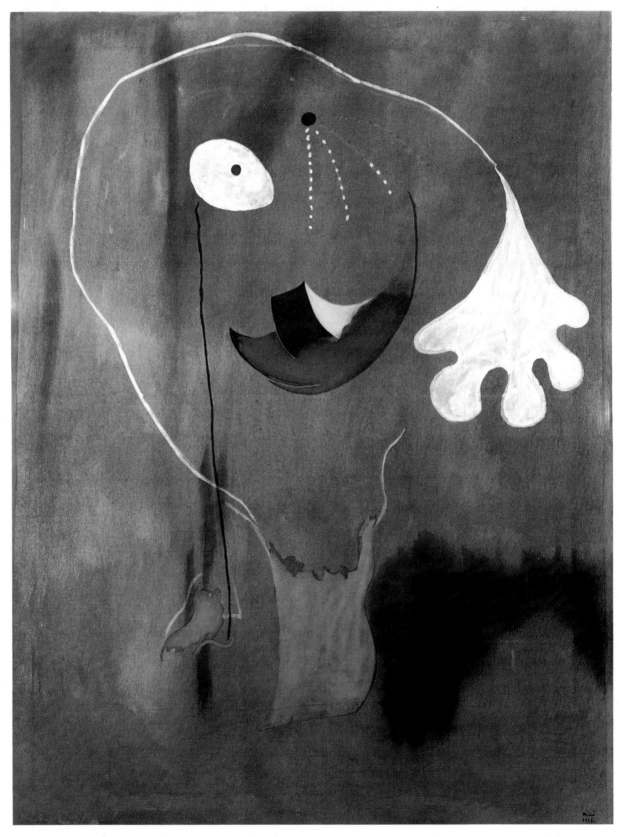

PAINTING, 1925
Oil, 45⁵/₈" x 35". Collection: Mr. and Mrs. Ralph F. Colin, New York

30

PAINTING, 1925
Oil, 51¹/₈" x 38¹/₈". Collection: Pierre Janlet, Brussels

TABLE WITH GLOVE, 1921. Oil, 46" x 35¹/₄"
Collection: Museum of Modern Art, New York (Gift of Armand G. Erpf)

THE MYTHOLOGICAL ARABESQUES OF CHILDHOOD

Proceeding by abrupt stops and starts, as was his custom, and profiting from the favorable solitude of Montroig, during the summer of 1923 Miró began work on several paintings, which he later patiently completed, and in which he intended to lucidly define the new positions adopted. He was not a man for improvisation or violent haste; despite the radical changes he introduced and the revolutionary attitude he cited as his authority, equilibrium always prevailed in his life. Breaking with the past, rejecting the possibilities offered by contemporary movements, and even disdaining intermediate solutions, with *The Tilled Field* and especially with *The Hunter,* he plunged with a single leap into that universe of play and magic henceforth destined to become his world and for which he very quickly found his own characteristic means of expression.

However, he embarked on this adventure in a state of complete awareness. On several occasions he related his experiment to his friend Rafols with perfect lucidity, and described to him the two principal paintings he was then working on: « I am succeding in escaping into the absolute of nature, and my landscapes have no connection with external reality... I know I am following dangerous roads, and I confess I am often seized with the panic of the traveler walking along unexplored paths. But then I react, thanks to the discipline and severity with which I am working. » A short time later, according to Dupin, he added: « Hard at work and full of enthusiasm. Monstrous animals and angelic animals. Trees with ears and eyes, and a peasant with a Catalan cap, holding a hunting gun and smoking his pipe. All pictorial problems solved. To express with precision all the golden sparks of our soul. »

There was in truth nothing more hazardous and risky for him than to decide suddenly to put aside the semblance of any prestige, revolutionize his ideas, and abandon solid ground in order to penetrate, as he expressed it, the heart of the most hidden and intimate reality. While giving up none of his passionate love for Montroig and his privileged knowledge of beings and objects, he instinctively turned to the realm of childhood, which he restores to us as if in a wondrous dream.

In *The Tilled Field* nothing is missing from this rendezvous with memory. Every object, every tree, plant, furrow, the farm, the familiar field and barnyard animals, even the jack-in-the-box leaping from his container, and the fragment of newspaper imitating a collage, appear in different proportions, decreased or enlarged by the dream. The picture, composed of superimposed registers and lightly modulated areas of colors that are soft and often rather dull, is very carefully composed in the manner of a tapestry. It matters little that he made use of certain reminiscences of popular art and the Gerona Apocalypse stored in his memory in order to accentuate the imaginary and liberate himself from these beribboned animals and decorative volutes as he desired. His success is undeniable, and the effect of surprise for the spectator invited to participate in the gaily decorated festival unfolding before his eyes is complete. While Catalonia is present in *The Hunter* through its symbols, emblems, and typical atmosphere, the distance crossed is larger, because the remnant of reality, as reflected in the form of even a fractionated or transposed image, has disappeared. The world is reduced to a state of geometric figures and outlines, serpentine lines, and leaping flames, and is simplified in an almost esoteric language, rigorously arranged in an atmosphere in which the smallest element is heavy with a magical or symbolic significance. The composition takes on the appearance of a visual incantation in which the artist is already spontaneously beginning to resurrect the old myths: Jacob's ladder linking earth and heaven, the opposition of the male and female principles, sun and moon, the omnipresence of sex converted into the fateful triangle, and so on.

Throughout that year Miró, putting to use the stimuli provided by Paris, exercised his agile style in defining and constructing his pseudopuppets in *Portrait of Madame X, Maternity,* and *Spanish Dancer,* freeing himself from his obsessions *(The Trap),* and adding to the alphabet of forms he was constantly creating, with the entertaining animation of a children's story or a picture puzzle *(The Toys, The Sommersault).* As was his usual practice, he quickly combined the experiences acquired into *Harlequin's Carnival,* a masterwork with ocher tonal values, in which figures, animals, objects, dancing flames, and symbols, assembled in a closed, suggestive space, come to life and move in rhythm, with a conspiratorial smile, in a painting reminiscent of a carefully choreographed ballet or a protocartoon.

In *Smile of My Blonde,* a short time later in « *Etoiles en des sexes d'escargot* », and « *Oh, un de ces Messieurs* », and even more visibly in *The Body of My Brunette,* Miró also frequently tries to combine the symbol with the word, to wed sculpture and language, repeating an experiment made in *The Hunter.* Here he was following the exhortations of his numerous poet friends, whose influence was now beginning to be felt.

He was already friendly with Tzara, one of whose books he later illustrated, and during his sojourns in the rue Blomet he had the opportunity to enjoy closer relations with most of the people who assiduously frequented Masson's studio: Limbour, Leiris, Desnos, Tual, Salacrou, Artaud, Jacques Prévert, and others. On occasion he also met better established writers and poets: Soupault, Breton, Ribemont-Dessaignes, Péret (who wrote the introduction to his next exhibition), Crevel, Aragon, and Eluard and others who had at first been associated with *Littérature,* and who in 1924 had just defined the position of their group in « Le Manifeste du Surréalisme » and the new magazine *La Révolution Surréaliste.*

During the period of the « sleeping sessions » he was able to attend some of the famous meetings in the studio in the Place Blanche, during which Crevel, Péret, and especially the inexhaustible Desnos made hypnotic speeches that were reproduced in *Littérature.* Unlike Masson, however, Miró did not derive immediate consequences for psychic automatism from these sessions. At that time he was satisfied to follow the example set by Apollinaire and Sonia Delaunay, often repeated in *Les Soirées de Paris,* by inserting his words or a phrase in a genuine structure (less rigid, however, than the one earlier adopted by Max Ernst in *Painting-poem*), permitting himself to fall into a cursive, animated rhythm reminiscent of the scrolls and streamers of the medieval tapestries and contemporary graffiti.

Above all, he took the favorable atmosphere, need for renewal, power granted to the imagination, and return to the miraculous extolled by the Surrealists as his authority for his own struggle, which he was waging in his always somewhat solitary way. Breton was not fooled. Although he joined the rest of the group in applauding Miró's one-man exhibition in 1925 at the Galerie Pierre and included him shortly thereafter in the first Surrealist exhibition, he only belatedly decided to praise the artist's work in his series of writings on *Le Surréalisme et la peinture,* and then only with many reservations and warnings. With quite prophetic accuracy of viewpoint, he states: « Joan Miró has perhaps a single desire, the desire to surrender himself, in order to paint and only to paint (which for him means confining himself to the one field in which we are certain he has the equipment), to that pure automatism... whose value and profound justification I fear Miró has very summarily verified. » In contrast, he was not for a moment thinking of our painter when he aptly mentioned the intervention of elements in the awakening of oneirism, although this was very important in Miró's work: « As children we had toys that today would make us cry with pity and rage. Who knows? Perhaps later we shall reexamine the toys of our entire life as we do those of our childhood... We continue to grow until a certain age, it seems, and our toys grow up with us. » Breton excommunicated the painter with alacrity for his participation, with Max Ernst, in the preparation during 1926 of the sets for *Romeo et Juliette* for Diaghilev's Ballets Russes.

Miró was not at all affected by these passing disagreements. On the contrary, his feelings were strengthened by his recent discovery of the work of Klee, whose astonishing faculty of poetic creation fascinated him, and by the support of Jacques Viot in selling his paintings and organizing his exhibition of June 12-27, 1925, at the Galerie Pierre. Here he was encouraged by the presence of his numerous friends at the vernissage and by the success obtained, despite the fact that it took a somewhat scandalous turn. Miró abandoned his magical diagrams, and until 1927 abandoned himself to pure spontaneity and the free outpouring of the dream, in accordance with the precepts decreed by the Surrealists.

He used two methods of freeing himself from a world of hallucinatory sensations, in which he seemed to revel freely while barely checking the irresistible flood. Sometimes he gives birth to strange ectoplasms, as difficult to grasp as phantasms, which mingle, couple, coil, and vanish in coils of smoke, only rarely giving way to definite silhouettes that are by turns droll or disturbing *(Lovers, A Smoker's Head, Lady Walking, Person and Horse, The Statue).* At other times he plunges into an abyss of reflection, or a desert, or toward an endless horizon upon which a minuscule signal, some point or outline, serves as a marker buoy *(Catalan Peasant, The Birth of the World),* and the richness of the elaborate backgrounds with their luminous blues and even whites fully reflects his joy in the face of this impression of emptiness and freedom — a justified cause of alarm for André Breton. However, in the summer calm of Montroig he as usual prepared the antidote for this revealing but excessive abandon. In 1926 and 1927 he patiently worked on several paintings that announce the discerningly chosen solution intermediate between visionary delirium and the simplicity of rule. Upon contact with his native soil, the absolute again becomes smiling and familiar, while retaining its enigmatic air and its instinctive grandeur, in that remarkable series of canvases — *Person Throwing a Stone at a Bird, Dog Barking at the Moon, The Grasshopper, The Hare, Nude,* and so on — that quickly became famous thanks to their contrasting areas of color and Miró's extreme power of suggestion and dream via a figuration that is restrained and ingenuous, but powerfully evocative.

With superb assurance he completed this chapter of his existence on a note of beauty, scoring successes in all aspects of his life. In 1927, thanks to Viot, he was able to settle in the Cité des Fusains in Montmartre's rue Tourlaque, where he found Eluard, Ernst, Arp, Magritte, and the effective stimulus of their proximity. His exhibition, organized through Pierre Loeb, in May 1928 at the Galerie Georges Bernheim accentuated his success, especially in view of the fact that Bernheim was a well-established gallery. Lastly, his marriage at Palma in October 1929 to Pilar Juncosa was, in the eyes of his family, the crowning point of his career.

Better still, a trip to Holland in the spring of 1928 inspired him to paint, during the summer and following months, very free interpretations of several of the works that had caught his attention in the museums. These works actually served merely as remote plastic references and pretexts for more or less similar rhythms in *Dutch Interior* and *The Potato* and in the imaginary portraits entitled *Portrait of Mrs. Mills* and the quite elliptical *Portrait of a Lady in 1820.* For Miró, what mattered was the clear definition, humanization, and increased integration into space of his ribbonlike forms, seemingly so whimsical but nevertheless developed in great detail to bloom at will, with an elegant slenderness, into a dazzling cascade of colors. However, this extremely successful series of canvases was shortly interrupted.

Miró very soon became disturbed in the face of this unbridled lyricism with its too predictable results and its too easily obtainable charm. In accordance with his usual disposition he sought to weaken his ties with his neighbors and to struggle against his environment. He moved to the rue François Mouton and contemplated a step backward, following the revolutionary Dada advice of earlier years and challenging the bases of painting in order to mock and more deeply examine himself. This lacerating and often painful examination was made between 1929 and 1931, a short time before the outbreak of the crisis that invited every human being to make a general reexamination of the age.

With courage and resignation he endured its consequences, which became increasingly difficult, to the point that in 1933 he was obliged to spend the entire year working in Barcelona. His situation was exacerbated by the presence in his life of his wife and his daughter Dolores, born in July 1931. However, with extraordinary tenacity he continued to explore the various possibilities of expression and materials, paying little heed to the unfavorable reception of the public and still less to that of the dealers, who were facing severe difficulties.

He appears so deeply motivated by a sudden exasperation, animated by a feeling

PAINTING
(THE CHECK),
1925
Oil,
76³/₄" x 51¹/₈"
Collection:
Pierre Matisse
Gallery, New York

Dog Barking at the Moon, 1926
Oil, 29" x 36¼"
Collection: Philadelphia Museum of Art, (A.E. Gallatin Collection)

LANDSCAPE, 1927
Oil, 51¹/₈" x ³/₄"
Collection: Mr. and Mrs. Gordon Bunshaft, New York

Circus Horse, 1927
Oil., 51¹/₈" x 38¹/₈
Private collection, Brussels

40

of self-destruction and dominated by a vehement need for provocation, that the violence of his behavior is startling. Beginning in 1928, with his first ironic, disillusioned *picture-objects* (*Spanish Dancer* is one example), he almost mocks his own experiments. In his collages of 1929 he abruptly and carelessly bestrews the blank paper with torn fragments of sandpaper or wrapping paper, and fills them in with shadowy lines. In his *Constructions* of 1930, he still more crudely assembles bits of debris and miscellaneous materials discovered at random. But as early as 1931 a relaxation appears in his more finished, poetic objects, in which ordinary locks and padlocks serve as piquant symbols. The disappearance of a large part of this rather ephemeral output, which was not highly valued at the time of its creation, is a pity, for it represents an important link in his work, and its degree of anticipation in relation to contemporary art makes it all the more valuable to us today.

Miró, however, was not traveling alone on this road. In 1933 Aragon succeeded in organizing at the Galerie Pierre a group exhibition based on a text entitled *Painting Issues a Challenge!*, which was to create great interest. The sculptor Giacometti, a new friend of Miró's, was traveling a similar path. He recognized that Miró was endowed with an extraordinary soundness of taste and was able to extricate himself skillfully from the most perilous positions.

Despite their dangerous nature and the fact that they caused an inevitable hiatus in his work, the experiments carried out during these four years were extremely profitable for him. They led him to eliminate the excesses of his instinctive eloquence and to prove his capabilities, and on the other hand they aroused in him a desire to return to discipline and the indispensable exuberance, while maintaining extreme simplicity of accent. Chiefly, however, they enabled him to dictate to his material in order to turn it into an instrument docile to his most daring and ambitious designs.

His strange paintings on paper, created between 1931 and 1933 under frequently difficult conditions, already testify to an undeniable maturity and power, and by their broad streams of color and free and authoritative style they herald lyrical abstraction. However, he put them aside in order to rediscover his fondness for the fantastic in several small paintings executed on wood in 1932 and for unself-conscious humor in several drawing-collages, created at the beginning of 1933 and rich in turn-of-the-century reminiscences.

At the end of this long detour, and basing his work on collages that served as inspirational motifs, to maintain his link with reality, he finally produced a major series of large paintings, executed in 1933 in Barcelona, despite the cramped conditions of his studio in the Pasaje del Credito, and exhibited very successfully in October at the Galerie Bernheim in Paris. He was finally in possession of an autonomous personal language that he was later to repeat on numerous occasions without any need to modify its absolute perfection. The play of elemental forms under his complete mastery, reinforced and elaborated by lines of equal simplicity, is inscribed within a boundless space, with superabundant energy, and with fiery colors that contrast or harmonize with carefully developed backgrounds, easily creating a unified work having a vivid and engaging majesty. In 1934 this led him to prepare a series of four tapestry cartoons and to paint three enormous wall

Study for the Portrait of Mistress Mills in 1750, 1929
Pencil on lined paper, 5¹/₄" x 4¹/₄". Collection: Museum of Modern Art, New York (Gift of the Artist)

42

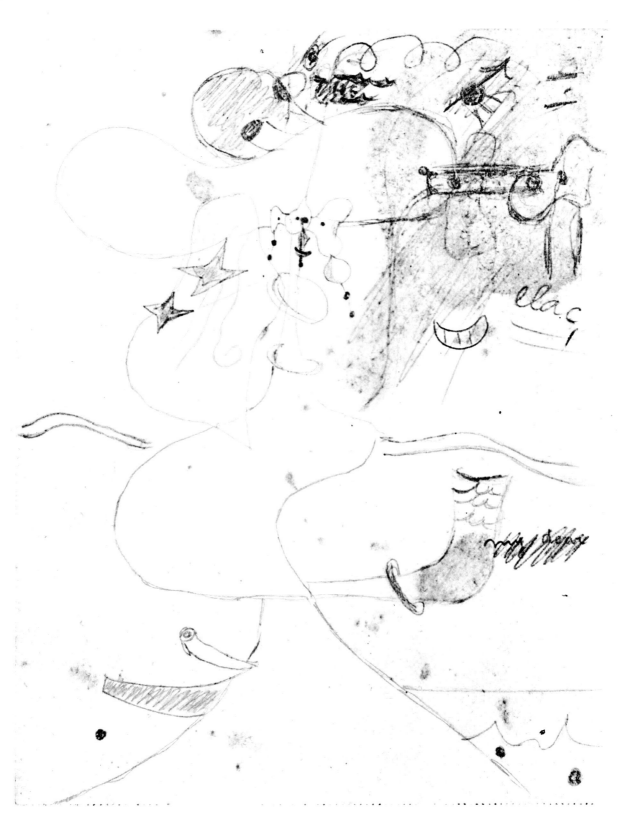

Study for the Portrait of Mistress Mills in 1750, 1929
Pencil, 8¹⁄₈″ x 6⁵⁄₈″. Collection: Museum of Modern Art, New York (Gift of the Artist)

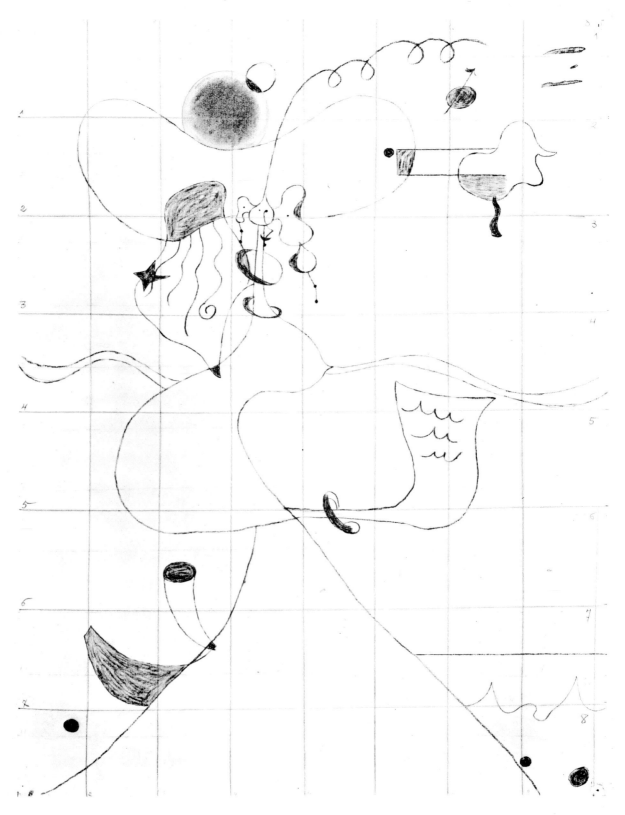

Cartoon for the Portrait of Mistress Mills in 1750, 1929
Charcoal and pencil, 24³/₄" x 19". Collection: Museum of Modern Art, New York (Gift of the Artist)

44

PORTRAIT OF MISTRESS MILLS IN 1750, 1929
Oil, 45$^1/_2$" x 35". Private Collection, New Canaan, Conn.

PAINTING, 1933. Oil, 57¹/₂" x 44⁷/₈". Collection: Mr. and Mrs. Klaus Perls, New York

PORTRAIT OF A LADY IN 1820, 1829. Oil, 45⅝" x 35". Private collection

DUTCH INTERIOR I, 1928. Oil 36^1/$_8$" x 28^3/$_4$"
Collection: Museum of Modern Art, New York (Mrs. Simon Guggenheim Fund)

Cartoon for Dutch Interior I, 1928
Charcoal and pencil, 24⁵/₈" x 18". Collection: Museum of Modern Art. New York

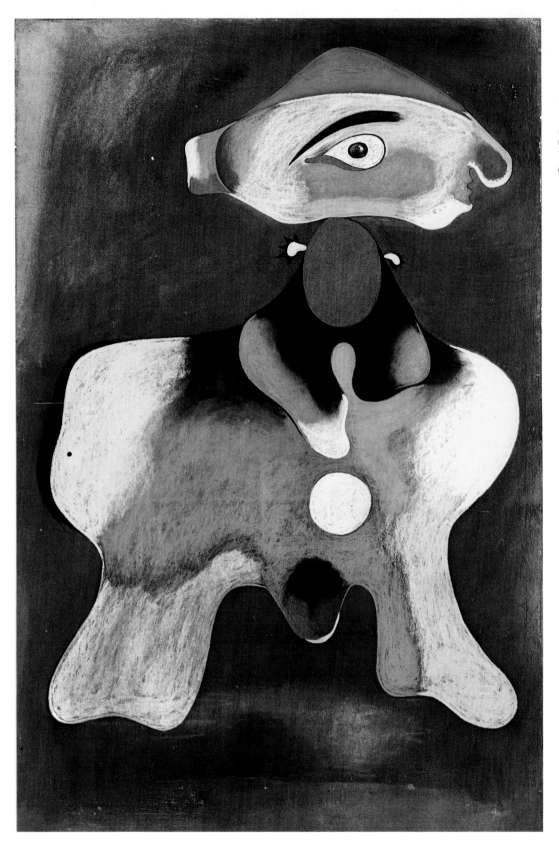

WOMAN, 1934
Pastel and
pencil on tan pape
41³/₄" x 27⁵/₈"
Collection:
Philadelphia
Museum of Art
(Louise and
Walter Arensberg
Collection)

HEAD OF A MAI
193
Gouache an
India ink c
black pape
25⁵/₈" x 19³/₄
Collectior
Richard S. Zeisle
New Yor

panels for Pierre Loeb. Starting with the sets for *Jeux d'enfants*, which he carefully designed in 1932 for the Ballets de Monte-Carlo, and continuing with the etchings that he began to engrave in 1933, Miró's inclination toward an art that was monumental in conception became increasingly stronger and indisputably triumphed. Unfortunately, in the succeeding years he was to have only a few opportunities to make use of it, notably for Madame Cuttoli, for the Spanish Pavilion at the World's Fair of 1937, for Pierre Matisse, and for the architect Paul Nelson.

THE APPEARANCE OF ANXIETY AND ITS ULTIMATE SUBLIMATION

In one of his habitual sudden shifts, Miró abruptly abandoned the solutions he had just found and adopted, as if he were obliged to answer a call originating from the depth of his consciousness. In 1934 he began to use pastels, and with a heightened power of suggestion presented monstrous, grimacing beings of unusual scope (*Woman, Person*). From this time on a muted anxiety, a secret premonition of the storms and catastrophes accumulating on the horizon, and a feeling for the tragic, which until then had not been very pronounced in his paintings, penetrated and riddled his work, causing certain violent distortions in the painting-collages on sandpaper to which he was greatly attached at this time. Anxiety creeps in, gains ground step by step, and becomes oppressive in numerous paintings of 1935 with their nightmarish forms, including *Persons in the Presence of Nature* with its dark coloration, *Two Persons,* composed of various elements and complex textures, and *Rope and People,* which he repeats in a kind of litany to avert doom. Ultimately this anxiety even suffocated and distorted the familiar, peaceful atmosphere of *The Farmers' Meal.*

Even before the outbreak of the tragic events of 1936 in Spain, in several paintings carefully worked out on copper or Masonite, sinister threats proliferate, the earth prepares to erupt, and monsters multiply, sowing terror on all sides (*Person Attracted by the Form of a Mountain, Persons and Mountains*). Haunted by some terrible foreboding of the catastrophes awaiting him, he turned to tar, bitumen, and sand, tracing exacerbated symbols in them. Soon, confined to Montroig in the summer while the civil war broke out, he began his descent into hell in his work, heaping up on Masonite panels splintered, violent forms that are outcries of pain or absolute denial in the face of the drama steeping his country in blood. In the fall he took refuge with his family in Paris, but he was helpless, unable to work because of his lack of lodging, and lost in the throng of exiles.

However, even before settling into a small apartment in the boulevard Blanqui, he quickly regained his foothold on reality — but a reality that nevertheless continued to be disfigured and maleficent, in drawings made from life in the Grande Chaumière, in the *Still Life with Old Shoe* painted with difficulty in Pierre Loeb's cellar, and, slightly later,

HELP SPAIN, 1937. Poster, stencil printed in color, 9³/₄" x 7⁵/₈"
Collection: Museum of Modern Art, New York (Gift of the Pierre Matisse Gallery)

54

Barcelona Series XLVII, 1944
Lithograph, 10" x 13"
Collection: Museum of Modern Art, New York

Barcelona Series XXIII, 1944
Lithograph, 24³/₈" x 18⁹/₁₆"
Collection: Museum of Modern Art, New York

ROPE AND PEOPLE I, 1935. Oil on cardboard mounted on wood, with coil of rope, 41$^1/_4$" x 29$^3/_8$"
Collection: Museum of Modern Art, New York (Gift of the Pierre Matisse Gallery)

in an unfinished *Self-portrait.* In these two canvases, visibly inspired by Van Gogh's example (for Miró too was assailed by his demons and preyed on by anguish mingled with pity), he clung to reality like a shipwrecked soul and eagerly examined it until he discovered the shadows and flames swirling about him, ready to devour the world.

This stormy wind continued to pursue him in 1937 and 1938, with brutal incandescences that cause horrible silhouettes and monstrous masses (*Two Women Surrounded by Birds, Group of Persons, Woman's Head*) to emerge from their darkness. Perhaps the sole exception is *The Reaper,* the now-destroyed monumental decoration painted on cellotex for the Spanish Pavilion, in which dignity triumphed over pathetic protest. However, there were brief intervals (*The Circus, Birdsong in Autumn*) that heralded the return of calm at the end of 1938, and the successful simplifications that intervened, within a short time of each other, between two of the versions of *Portrait,* the tormented, still ambiguous version in the Baltimore Museum, and the very relaxed version in the Zürich Kunsthaus, and between the two equally different interpretations of *Seated Woman.*

While the confusion into which he was plunged by the Spanish tragedy remained unchanged, he eluded its temporal development and the event itself, and gradually became reabsorbed in the frenzied labor of the artist. As an artist he participated by his submissions in the manifestations organized throughout the world in honor of Surrealism: Copenhagen, Teneriffe in 1935, London and New York in 1936, Japan in 1937, Paris in 1938, Mexico in 1940. His one-man exhibitions presented annually in New York, beginning in 1932, by the Pierre Matisse Gallery, enjoyed a growing success that was to be crowned by the 1941-1942 retrospective at the Museum of Modern Art, arranged by J. J. Sweeney.

Thus he was better equipped to resist the growing tension of the age, fend off new blows of fate, and achieve complete detachment from what was happening around him, without, however, resigning himself to indifference or forgetfulness. In defiance of the terrible circumstances through which he was passing, he was preoccupied solely with this encounter with himself and his art, communicating to the latter that desire to excel which motivated and guided him, and which he succeeded in elevating to a level hitherto unattained.

On the eve of World War II, benefiting from several short trips to Varengeville (where he stayed with the architect Nelson), in his series *Bird in Flight above the Plain,* with its powerful dynamism and its untrammeled lightness, he already reveals a desire to banish threats and apprehensions, to stand aloof, and to shun the commonplace. Permanently installed from August 1939 to May 1940 in the same seacoast locality, where he rented a house (the « Clos des Sansonnets ») not far from Braque, he enjoyed the calm, starry nights, listened to records, and abandoned himself to intensive work, permitting himself no distraction. An ingenuous smile begins to brighten the figures of his first nocturnes painted on red backgrounds. Soon his élan was accentuated and rediscovered the path of symbols as a means of masterfully evoking creatures and birds mingled with stars in a solid rhythmic interlacing bestrewn with scumbled flashing forms that stand out against the sackcloth he used to emphasize the almost magically visionary appearance (*The Ladder Escape*).

Dawn soon appeared at the end of this long night. Promises were transformed into genuine masterpieces in the series of 23 gouaches and paintings created in the same spirit and the same modest dimensions between January 1940 and September 1941, under the completely justified title of *Constellations*. To be sure, the maleficent figuration has not completely disappeared, but it now occupies only an infinitely small place; it is absorbed into the immensity of a subtly gray-toned space, punctuated by a multitude of stellar images strung together, as if in a necklace, in supple, leaping, graphic interlacings (*The Beautiful Bird Explaining the Unknown to the Pair of Lovers, Toward the Rainbow*). An encompassing, smiling music of the spheres emanates from these works, in which Miró appears to have attained a genuine Nirvana, diametrically opposed to the warlike furies of the age. From first to last, the same enchanting spectacle unfolds: stars, the sun, the moon, various symbols, defined by very vivid primary colors or blacks and hung on the links of a rhythmic, alternating ensemble, dance in the firmament like comets' tails or kites. Their sometimes almost interminable lines stretch out and unwind in serpentine coils, taking flight in a pearly string of confident cadences that are every bit the equal of the music of Mozart being enjoyed at this moment by our author. What better means could Miró have found to escape from the wounds being inflicted upon him, and to forget the painful stages of an exodus that forced him to flee with his family from Varengeville to Paris, then to Vich, to Palma, and finally to Montroig?

A calm spell followed this period of tenacious effort to dominate events and fully accomplish the task he had set for himself with admirable constancy. Encouraging news coming from New York also predisposed him toward a relaxation that had become indispensable to him in the solitary seclusion in which he had buried himself in Palma and Barcelona, which again became his residence after 1942. However, the numerous drawings, sometimes pastels, created during these years, and the small paintings that reappeared in 1944 accompanied by works that were more elaborate although painted on ordinary pieces of fringed cloth, all of which were based on the same tirelessly repeated theme of *Woman-Bird-Sun,* reveal a certain gravity and depth of spirit under their seeming spontaneity. This scale, constantly repeated like an exercise in style, enabled him to strengthen his repertoire and enrich his grammar of forms. At the same time it became an instrument of elevation, a chant of entreaty, and, by its mythical subject, a kind of prayer of intercession between earth and heaven, an orientation that coincides to a certain extent with his religious readings, particularly Saint John of the Cross, and with the death of his mother.

It is not astonishing that upon his arrival, early in 1945, at the end of this continual ascent, and without even waiting for the end of the war, he undertook with renewed fervor and dazzling ease the cycle of his large paintings that are certainly among the most successful of his career: *Women and Birds in the Night, Woman Listening to Music, The Bullfight.* By a stripping away of the superfluous, allied with an instinctive refinement, he effortlessly obtained a language that is of classical purity by virtue of the fullness and firmness of its style, the amplitude of its forms, the rigorous sobriety of its harmonies with their melodious brilliancy, and the very power of a visionary world, totally and actually re-created. In a cosmos punctuated with stars and various symbols, among which the eyes and the sexes are of major importance, human beings and imaginary animals stand out with majestic elegance while remaining linked to the linear movement of the whole, which is accentuated by the light and dark (sometimes black) alternations of the backgrounds. Dynamism and simplifications unfold, paralleling an insistent humor, during the following year (*Women at Daybreak*).

The taste for the monumental that prompted him to begin working in ceramics with Artigas in 1944, and to return to sculpture in 1945, asserted itself so strongly that soon he was receiving orders for murals, one in 1947 for a large mural for the Terrace Plaza Hotel in Cincinnati (which gave him an opportunity to spend some time in the United States), and a commission in 1948 for a smaller mural for Joaquim Gomis in Barcelona, which he executed in the same spirit as his paintings of 1945. The doors of the future were now fully opened to him.

A RADIANT, TRIUMPHANT PRIMITIVISM

Miró entered upon a new and final stage after the war with his trips in 1947 to New York, where he remained for eight months, and in 1948 to Paris, where his return, hailed by all his friends, was transformed into a glorious event when his exhibition opened in November at the Galerie Maeght. He had finally emerged from his long seclusion in Spain, and was meeting with a recognition that was to galvanize his efforts in the coming years.

The monumental (33″ × 10″) painting he successfully completed for the Cincinnati hotel, the frieze he executed during the same period for the International Surrealist Exhibition in Paris, and his rediscovery of old friends in both cities revived his desire to set to work with greater assurance and to test his ability with larger formats and different materials. He took advantage of this desire to learn copperplate engraving in Hayter's New York studio and color lithography on Mourlot's presses in Paris. Above all, he discovered the bracing American environment, which invited him to take more daring liberties and to renew his interest in the Far East, which was then enjoying a vogue in the United States.

The first indications of this change of orientation can barely be felt in the works painted at the beginning of 1948, although they are characterized by the greater importance sometimes given to humor, a naïve awkwardness, and violent colors (*The Moon, The Red Sun Eats the Spider*). Over the years he retained his tested and proven, detailed, orderly technique; in several works of 1949-1950, highly colored, schematic silhouettes inserted into a supple, melodic graphic network unfold on an extremely palpable background, as in the painting with acrobatic figures in the Kunsthaus of Zürich, or the work with the amusing elongated face in the Tate Gallery in London. This is even more striking in his murals, which become increasingly simplified, beginning with the work he completed in 1951 for the

Harvard Graduate School in Cambridge, and including the admirable Wall of the Sun and Wall of the Moon, built of ceramic in 1957, with the help of Artigas, for UNESCO in Paris, and the 1961 wall panel painted for J. L. Sert.

However, Miró showed an increasing impatience to express himself in a more spirited and eloquent style, in which he plays, with supreme mastery, with such unusual materials as wire, sealing wax, string, and other materials. Finally, in 1950, he created his picture-objects on canvas, cardboard, and Masonite, which he sometimes dug out with a gouge and finished off with small objects picked up at random. In *Painting with Ropes* (Lindhoven Museum), the surface is covered like a mortar, and with its colored clouds blooming with miscellaneous bits of debris it resembles a genuine proto-tachism dominated by the authoritative emergence of a very orientalized symbol. The size and brutality of a black style that comes close to being elemental continued to increase between 1950 and 1952 (*Cry of the Gazelle at Daybreak, The Mauve of the Moon Covers the Green of the Frog, Bird with a Calm Gaze, Its Wings Aflame*), approaching its peak in 1953 with the violent spontaneity of primitive incantation in the painting in the Guggenheim Museum, and in 1954 with the proliferation of outlines of hands and signs on a red background, as in *Hope Returns through the Flight of the Constellations*. Sometimes he surrounds the savage graffiti with a kind of luminous punctuation that slightly softens the harshness of the contours and the huge hands (*Coiffeur Disheveled by the Flight of Constellations, The Caresses of the Gleam of the Moon*).

The influence of the Far East even prompted him to venture into the pure evanescence of simply elliptical black or colored splotches (with which he obtained a series of remarkable successes in 1952 by totally stripping them of all superfluous material), and in 1953 to launch into the painting of horizontal and vertical stripes several yards long, covered with a kind of calligraphy reminiscent at close range of oriental scrolls.

Through the power of this creative instinct that surged up and exploded within him, he came to take greater satisfaction from his battle with materials — ceramic, lithography, engraving, and so on. He devoted most of his time to this activity, to the point of abandoning painting until 1960 and organizing an exhibition in June 1956 at the Galerie Maeght, consisting solely of his *grand feu* pottery made at Gallifa with the assistance of Artigas and his son.

He was also greatly absorbed in work for his UNESCO commission and his second visit to the United States in 1959 for his major retrospective at the Museum of Modern Art, and lastly and especially in the installation of the large studio he had wanted for so many years, built by his friend J. L. Sert on the slope of the Calamayor Hill in Palma de Majorca.

Bringing this long period of not painting to an end, he set to work again with the impetuosity of youth, despite his 67 years, and as usual made ready to reexamine all the pictorial solutions he had previously selected. The temptation to do so was made all the stronger by the fact that thanks to his ceramic and etching work he had just acquired certain practices that he now intended to put to use in painting.

He explored his previous methods more deeply and made several modifications in

STILL LIFE WITH OLD SHOE, 1937
Oil, 32¹/₄" x 46"
Collection: Museum of Modern Art, New York (Gift of James Thrall Soby)

WOMEN AND BIRDS IN THE NIGHT, 1944
62   Oil, 28⁵/₁₆" x 20³/₈". Collection: Yale University Art Gallery, New Haven, Conn.

PERSONAGES AND STAR, 1949. Oil, 25¹/₂" x 20"
Collection: Mr. and Mrs. Ralph F. Colin, New York

« Le Cirque », 1937. Oil on calotex, 47³/₄" x 35³/₄"
Collection: The Meadows Museum, Southern Methodist University, Dallas, Texas

them. The spirit of meditation and asceticism inspired in him by his admiration for the Far East was carried to its ultimate consequences after 1960. With visible pleasure, and using the simplest methods of light scumblings on cardboard in preference to canvas, he plunged at times into the diluted white areas of a space demarcated with fragile markers — glimmers, stains, outlines, speckles, and so on — at other times into clouds lighted up by the presence of a star (*Solitude, The Red Disc*). At still other times he used a refined *tachisme,* from which there emerge vague silhouettes (*Man and Woman in the Sun*) and, more often, fragile signs (*Birds in Space*) and fragmentary (*Writing on Red Background*) or elemental (*Seated Woman*) calligraphies. By 1961 he was creating several immense, completely purified mural paintings — *Blue I, II,* and *III,* all of a luminous blue bestrewn with flaming comets' tails and dark stars. From time to time he returns with delight to this evocation of an ethereal dream and a calm interior universe haloed with the apprehensive tenderness of a poet, the product of a dual need for a closely blended preciosity and purification, as in his 1968 paintings *Flight of the Dragonfly before the Sun, The Star Smiles at the Twin Tree of the Plain.*

However, violence often reclaims its former rights. A truly expressive fury unfurls in an increasingly succinct and compact style and takes root in and dominates his work, beginning in 1960 with *Man and Woman in a Landscape* and *Bird's Head,* in which the black paint spreads out in thick outlines, stains, splotches, and projections. Miró was encouraged in this direction by his then current work directly on the tiles without preliminary preparation. In the succeeding years its scope broadened and it gained in barbaric, almost savage power, in 1963 with *Woman's Head* and *Bird on a Beautiful Blue Day, Person and Birds,* and in 1965 with *Blue Head and Bird-Arrow,* in which flashes of pigment gleam among the dark masses and energetic outlines.

Even in his vast and increasingly well-ordered compositions, such as *Friend's Message* of 1964 (the riddle of which has been so well explained by Yvon Taillandier), *Queen Marie Louise of Prussia* of 1965, and *Skiing Lesson* of 1966, the intensity of the color areas is restrained, like the fragments of a dazzling stained glass window, within vigorous structures, checkerboards, interlacings, and outlines in which the skillfully measured proportions of black areas in relation to the backgrounds heighten the suggestive power of the ideogram.

The symbol, reduced to its essence, remains supreme, occupies the leading place, and plays a determining symbolic role, in accordance with the traditions of primitive magic. It reappears in most of Miró's major creations of this period, in his powerfully monumental paintings *Women and Birds in the Night* and *Woman with Three Hairs, Surrounded by Birds in the Night,* and in his two mural ceramics with their accentuated dynamism of movement: one (*Alicia*) created for the Guggenheim Museum in 1967, and the other in the following year, to complete the vast ensemble gradually built up in the labyrinth he had conceived and peopled with his sculptures at the Fondation Maeght in Vence. There is no doubt that his trip to Japan in 1966 for his major retrospective greatly assisted in reinforcing his feelings concerning this preponderance of symbols.

THE POETESS, 1940
Gouache and oil wash on paper, 15" x 18¹/₈"
Collection: Mr. and Mrs. Ralph F. Colin, New York

66

Having reached the peak of his art many years earlier, and having created out of nothing a style that has proved to be accessible to everyone, Miró has completed a dazzling demonstration of his genius and qualities. Motivated by a frenetic activity, and endowed with a prodigious capacity for creation, in the past ten years, thanks to remarkably organized teamwork, he has succeeded in coping with an unprecedented accumulation of exhibitions and commissions. The Fondation Maeght, inaugurated in 1964, has helped him to become internationally famous, to fulfill the numerous demands made upon him, and to coordinate and develop his activity in various fields, by providing a complete summary of his work.

His native city of Barcelona gave a sumptuous welcome to his work in 1968 and commissioned a large monument for the Cervantes Gardens and later an immense ceramic work for its airport, executed in 1970.

Miró, an inexhaustible inventor endowed with overflowing vitality, is still able to surprise and arouse the enthusiasm of his audience, as was evident during his 1971 exhibition at the Fondation Maeght of his most recent works, including *Woman and Bird in the Night, Person* painted on newspaper, and other paintings whose exacerbated lyricism, blazing colors, and decisive symbolic power emphasized the soundness of the movement. More recently, in the presentation of his *Sobreteixims,* his prodigious fertility in making use of scraps of cloth and sacking created an astonishingly festive atmosphere of melodious dissonances in the Galerie Maeght.

We can be sure that every spectator of the extensive retrospective and particularly the ballet Miró is working on for 1974 will have the pleasure of rediscovering the infinite richness of this language he has created.

A GROWING INFLUENCE

With his characteristic fondness for stubborn, tireless labor, Miró has succeeded in continuously developing his conquest of other fields, a conquest that, as we have indicated, has kept pace with his painting. Especially during the last decade, he has come to play a leading role and to occupy a place without equal in contemporary art. His sculptural activity in particular has expanded considerably, until it now rivals the rest of his work in importance.

Although he was obliged for a long time, because of circumstances, to postpone the fulfillment of a sculptural vocation predicted as early as 1930 by Carl Einstein on the basis of the artist's « collage-objects » and « constructions, » Miró subsequently made up for lost time, thanks to the support give him by the Fondation Maeght. Availing himself of an incomparable craftsmanly sensibility, he felt a desire to come to grips with matter directly, to adopt a great variety of materials, and, long before others thought of using them in the name of their sociological context, to leave his stamp on the most ordinary objects destined to be discarded. Here, above and beyond the familiar irony from which he rarely deviates as a method of combating (by his own admission) his profound pessimism, he can continue to claim kinship with a total feeling of liberty in accordance with the Dadaist concepts that he had earlier been among the few to practice with a similar destructive violence, in the company of Man Ray, Picasso, and chiefly Giacometti with his *Apollo* and *Man, Woman, Child,* which were blazing the trail. Still better, he reveals a now very evident pleasure in liberating himself from his obsessions and exorcising his ghosts and secret phantasms by his frenzied imagination. Above all, I believe he has had the opportunity, first in his heads and terracotta birds, and then in his large figures with their combinations of textures, to abandon himself to the exhilaration of the poetic dream finally embodied in concrete form, to re-create the tutelary divinities and the eternal myths as he pleases, and later, by transforming perishable materials and found objects into bronze, to bring from his childhood memories a resurgence of the joys of hunting for intoxicating discoveries in the inexhaustible resources of nature.

He began his venture with ceramics between 1944 and 1950, backed by the experience and technical knowledge of his longtime friend Josep Llorens Artigas and, later, of the latter's son Joan. Here he discovered an unexpected joy in the possibility of having a direct link with his native soil, of lovingly working it with his fingers, and of spreading over its surface, almost by blind chance, colors that would appear only after firing. With his very first works, in his terracotta *Head* and *Figure,* his *Lunar Bird* and *Solar Bird* (also from 1944 - 46), immediately transposed into bronze and subsequently enlarged in marble or bronze, his various bronze statues entitled *Woman* (1949), his granite *Head,* his series of unusual found objects, the *Sculpture-objects* of 1950, made of a combination of materials as in the *Project for a Monument* (1954) with its provoking humor, he instinctively returns to the symbolic forms of the goddess-mother, fertility, and the initiation rites of the archaic Mediterranean and Andean civilizations.

His growing mastery of ceramics was obtained thanks to the major mural commissions he received at this time. After 1951 he also benefited from Artigas's move to the little village of Gallifa, with its more suitable atmosphere. Particularly between 1953 and 1956 Miró's skill developed in the direction of a craft production in the popular vein — dishes, vases, and so on — which he exhibited at this time, and culminated in 1962 - 63 in the large pieces — *Masque, Woman, Monument to Maternity, Man and Woman, Woman and Bird* — in which he made his well-known habitual innovations by using a variety of materials (stumps and roots of trees, metal, faience, fireclay, plaster, cork) which he transformed, cut out, assembled, engraved, and painted.

This feeling for the monumental, so dear to him, simultaneously reached its apogee in sculpture thanks to the establishment of the Fondation Maeght in Saint-Paul-de-Vence.

THE ESCAPE LADDER, 1940
Gouache and oil on paper, 15" x 18¹/₈"
Collection: Mrs. George Acheson, New York

THE MOON, 1948
Oil, 27$^1/_2$" x 36"
Collection: Mr. Charles Zadok, Greenwich, Conn.

THE RED SUN, 1948
Oil, 35$^7/_8$" x 28
Collection: The Phillips Gallery, Washington, D.C.

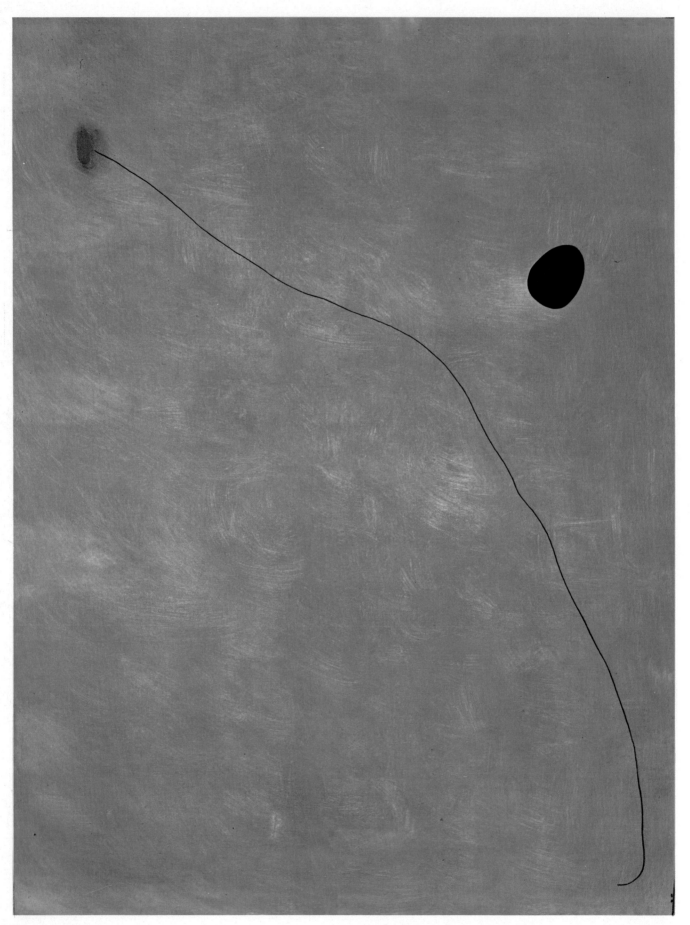

BLUE III, 1961. Oil, 106¹/₄″ x 139³/₄″. Collection: Pierre Matisse Gallery New York

This was an extremely intoxicating stimulant for him. Inevitably Miró was tempted to take advantage of this exceptional opportunity offered him, this unique framework carefully reconciled with his views by his faithful friend, the architect José Luis Sert, by establishing the museum he wanted in order to implant the full unfolding of his dreams on a grand scale. In 1963 he erected over the access road the majestic mass of *The Arc,* made of very carefully prepared concrete, and the tall allegorical silhouette of the bronze *The Fork.* Along the facades he placed the powerful silhouettes of the *grand-feu* ceramic *Goddess-Mother.* In subsequent years he added two birds, the *Totem,* the *Great Lizard,* and the *Young Girl in Flight,* done in glowing colors, and populated the labyrinth provided for this purpose with his creations.

After 1966 Miró, full of enthusiasm, completely abandoned himself to a prodigiously fertile creative process which made demands upon his personal ingenuity and the great skill of the teams best equipped to follow his daring instructions in the Paris foundries of Susse and Clementi, and particularly the Parellada foundry in Barcelona. He incorporated, united, and combined forms and materials in the constant variations at which he excelled, in order to achieve in his bronze castings (often colored) his customary poetic transmutation of combinations of the extremely incongruous objects he found and used: a carton, a chest, shards, cover, pitcher, umbrella, rod, stool, and so on. He displays a truly incomparable verve, liberty, irony, and eloquence in these numerous pieces created in recent years, most of which have womanhood as their theme. His found objects, which are in most cases very unusual, have become famous, especially in Spain with its traditional baroque spirit and humor. Lately he has not hesitated to use painted synthetic resin, which enables him to create larger masses than are possible with bronze and ceramic.

After 1969 Miró boldly launched into direct sand casting of very beautiful bas-reliefs in which he skillfully combines relief and intaglio impressions of objects and materials, in particular pellets of clay sometimes cast separately, linear bulges, and various engraved symbols obtained by using wet sand. In this brilliant display of pyrotechnics, sculptor and painter combine and complement each other to a supreme degree.

This feeling for line originates in a profound and constant need. Having been encouraged by Marcoussis to do engraving, Miró soon began to frequent Hayter's Atelier 17 in the rue Campagne Première. However, his graphic work did not really develop until after the war and burst into full bloom quite late, in keeping with the new possibilities available. For him this was definitely not just a simple outlet, as was the case with the tapestry work he did on several occasions when he had the use of the facilities of Sant Cugat's studio. As he told Yvon Taillandier, he wanted to express himself in all media. But for Miró as for Picasso, graphism was the preferred medium, the essential element, indispensable because of its speed, effectiveness, its elliptical and secret nature, and the absolute liberty it incarnates.

Chiefly to fill the requests of his poet friends for illustrations of their works, in 1930 he began his first, rather summary lithographs for Tristan Tzara's *L'arbre des voyageurs.* Shortly thereafter he tackled drypoint, and in 1933 he did the etchings for

WOMAN AND BIRD, 1963
Gouache on paper, $29^1/_8$" x $41^9/_{16}$". Private collection

74

Vase, 1966
38⁵/₁₆" High
Collection: Galerie
Maeght, Paris

Woman and Bird,
1968
Painted bronze,
108⁵/₆"x35¹/₄"x20"
Collection:
Galerie Maeght,
Paris

PERSONAGE AND BIRD IN FRONT OF THE SUN, 1963.
Oil on cardboard, 41³/₄" x 29¹/₄". Private collection

78

PERSONAGE AND BIRD, 1963. Oil on cardboard, 41³/₄" x 29¹/₄".
Private collection

79

WOMAN AND BIRD I, 1964
Oil, 83" x 83". Collection of the Artist

Ceramic plate, 1950
Private collection

81

82

Woman and Bird 1967
Bronze, 50¹/₄" x 22¹/₂"
Collection:
Galerie Maeght, Paris

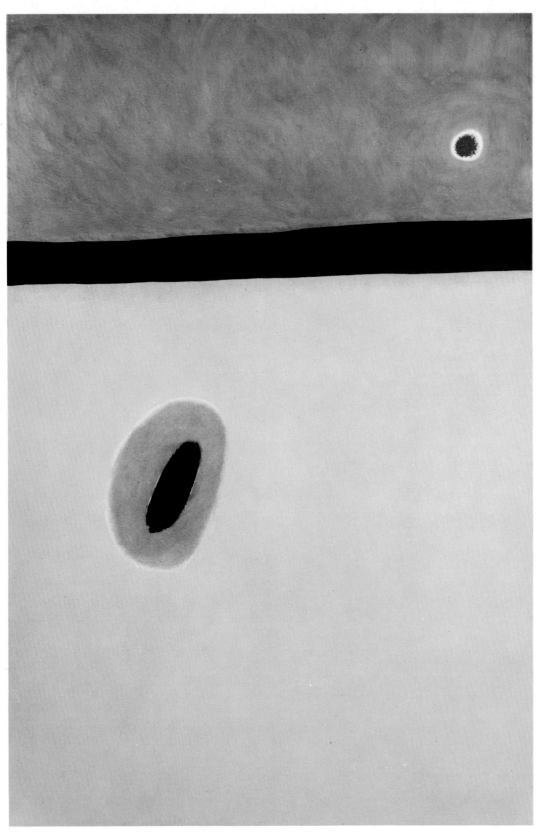

THE LARK'S WING
ENCIRCLED WITH
GOLDEN BLUE
REJOINS
THE HEART OF
THE POPPY
SLEEPING IN THE
DIAMOND-STUDDED
MEADOW,
Oil, 76$^7/_8$" x 51$^1/$
Collection:
Pierre Matisse Ga
New York

Georges Hugnet's *Enfances,* printed at Lacourière's plant. Subsequently he did several covers for *Minotaure, Transition,* and *L'usage de la Parole,* and etchings for booklets by Alice Paalen and Benjamin Péret. At Montroig in 1941, following Braque's advice and by force of circumstances, he began his vast series *Barcelona,* using lithographic crayon on transfer paper. But not until 1947 - 1948 did he begin a major, genuinely creative effort.

In New York Miró renewed his relationship with Hayter's Atelier 17, where he strengthened his technique and devoted himself with such spirit to etching that he very quickly completed the illustrations for Tzara's *L'antitête* and produced enough work to warrant a survey of his activity by Michel Leiris. In the following year a much broader field of activity opened up to him in Paris, where the Galerie Maeght invited him to contribute frequently to the *Cahiers* « Derrière le Miroir, » and published both an album of lithographs and Tzara's *Parler seul,* copiously illustrated. Miró participated closely in the work of Mourlot's shop, and constantly increased his authority, mastery, independence, and craftsmanly skill in combining methods and producing unexpected results. A survey exhibition of his prodigious labor in this domain was prepared in 1957 and triumphantly traveled throughout Germany. Shortly thereafter he returned masterfully to wood engraving, with the help of Enric Tormo, for Eluard's *A toute épreuve,* and in 1964, in connection with the *Ubu Roi* printed by Tériade, he adopted a monumental lithograph format with robust color areas.

The Fondation Maeght brought all his hopes to fruition by making space available to him in which he could work at his ease, surrounded by the odor of printer's ink of which he was so fond, by skilled and devoted technicians whom he quickly welded into a team to work with him, and later by a huge press on which he could make 120 x 160 prints. With this equipment he was able to devote himself more fully, with enthusiasm and dynamism, to an intensive lithographic output which he used with superb mastery, achieving dazzling feats of technical skill with the help of his assistants, and even the publication elsewhere, in 1971, of his own book of poems, *Le lézard aux plumes d'or.*

Ultimately the image which will probably be handed down to posterity, and which will soon be reflected in the Fundación Joan Miró officially established in May 1971 in Barcelona (with, once again, the assistance of José Luis Sert) will be that of a prodigious modern master of thinking and especially of seeing, an initiator and very often a disinterested inventor of methods of expression that have given birth to most of the major contemporary currents. In contrast to other artists who do not disdain to act like stars, Miró the man has always discreetly taken a back seat (as has been so well analyzed by Yvon Taillandier in his penetrating text *Je travaille comme un jardinier*) to Miró the prodigious artist capable of dominating his epic in a great variety of fields.

Throughout this visual festival which he has constantly guided and renewed, we prefer to think of him in the role of poet and creator combined in the guise of the magician capable of demonstrating continuing youthfulness of spirit and transmuting and transforming even materials regarded as worthless and uninteresting. These two skills are moreover closely linked, for Miró has almost miraculously succeeded in preserving his

WOMAN WITH THREE HAIRS SURROUNDED BY BIRDS IN THE NIGHT, 1972
Oil, 95⁷/₈" x 66¹/₂". Collection: Museum of Modern Art, New York (Gift of the Artist)

capacity for the enthusiasm and wonder engendered in us by the discoveries of childhood. In our civilization, aged by customs and overrun by excessive mechanization, this return to the original sources and appearances of spontaneity which we impute to the people of Prehistory and to the Primitives, and these rediscoveries made with seductive (if somewhat precious) ingenuousness, have been joyfully welcomed and judged by most people to be a genuine liberation. Despite the frequent presence of the tragic stamp of menacing silhouettes, every spectator rightly feels a message of hope and consolation in the ardent outburst of symbols reinvented with a rare mastery and in the singing, skillfully distributed colors. This is the song of the poet rising, with remarkable majesty, in a celebration of eternal youth and a proclamation of the wedding of heaven and earth, an identification with the liberating fugue, and above all the suggestion of the always-hoped-for escape toward the infinite spaces and imaginary immensities propitious to meditation. It is also the unparalleled magnitude displayed, in the fullness of age, by a creative genius endowed with inexhaustible fertility, and still more the consummation of a human will acting and intelligently playing a role within the difficult arcana of oneirism.

Above and beyond the goals set by the Dadaists and Surrealists, Miró alone has achieved the total accomplishment and even monumental insertion, in all its forms and in every material, of the dream inscribed — I would almost say installed — in the hearts of our cities, universities, and museums as well as in humble homes, like a touching and significant revelation of the new age.

GASTON DIEHL

SOBRETEIXIM XVII, 1973
94¹/₂ x 56"
Collection: Miró
Foundation, Barcelona

BIOGRAPHY

1893. Miró born on April 20 at 4 Pasaje del Credito in Barcelona, to a jeweler-clockmaker.

1900. Begins his studies at the nearby school at 13 Calle Regomir. Is an indifferent student, but is already extremely fond of drawing, which talent he practices in Majorca and near Tarragona.

1907. Registers at the Business School and the « La Llotja » School of Fine Arts.

1910. Having had no success at either school, is employed as an accounting clerk for Dalmau & Oliveras Co.

1911. Is attacked by nervous depression and typhoid fever. Profits by his convalescence at Montroig to return to drawing.

1912. Is permitted to register at the « Art School » run by Francesco Gali, who is able to awaken and guide his vocation. Becomes friends with his comrades E. C. Ricart and J. Llorens Artigas.

1915. Shares a studio with Ricart, and frequents the San Lluc Art Club, where he becomes acquainted with Joan Prats. J. F. Rafols, and others.

1917-18. Barcelona becomes the center of a growing artistic activity (Picabia publishes his magazine *391* here), in part thanks to the Dalmau Gallery, where Miró has his first exhibition.

1919. Joins the « Agrupacio Courbet. » Short visit to Paris, where he meets Picasso.

1920-21. Henceforth divides his time between Paris during the winter and Montroig during the summer. One-man show at the Galerie La Licorne, with introduction written by Raynal.

1922-25. Now installed in a studio in the rue Blomet, near André Masson's studio. Is in constant touch with the future Surrealists Breton, Aragon, and Eluard, and with Hemingway, Artaud, and Prévert. His exhibition at the Galerie Pierre, with introduction written by Péret, is extremely successful. Participates in the Surrealist demonstrations.

1926. Works with Max Ernst on the sets for *Romeo and Juliette,* despite the Surrealists' excommunication of him.

1928-31. The exhibition organized by Pierre Loeb at the Galerie Georges Bernheim establishes his reputation. In 1929 in Palma, marries his cousin Pilar Juncosa. Their daughter, Dolores, is born in July 1931.

1932. Exhibits in Paris at the Galerie Pierre Colle and in New York at the Pierre Matisse Gallery, which actively supports him.

1933-38. Has various exhibitions, and participates in shows in Paris, New York, Copenhagen, Teneriffe, London, and Tokyo. Leaves Spain. Works on the decoration for the Pavilion of the Republic of Spain at the Paris World's Fair.

1939-40. Takes refuge first at Varangeville, then (after the German invasion) at Majorca, Montroig, and Barcelona. His situation is precarious.

1941. Retrospective at the Museum of Modern Art in New York.

1942-44. Intensive work. Begins to work in ceramics, with Artigas. Death of his mother.

1945. Exhibition at the Galerie Vendôme in Paris.

1947. Trip to the United States.

1948. Major and rightly publicized presentation of his work (paintings and ceramics) at the Galerie Maeght, which later organizes many exhibitions on a regular basis.

1949. Exhibits in Barcelona, Stockholm, Berne, and Basel.

1954. International Grand Prize for engraving at the Venice Biennial. Until 1959 devotes most of his effort to ceramics.

1956. Retrospectives in Brussels, Amsterdam, Basel. Moves into a new studio in Palma.

1959. International Grand Prize of the Guggenheim Foundation. Trip to the United States for his retrospective at the Museum of Modern Art and in Los Angeles.

1960-61. Ceramic mural for Harvard University, shown in Barcelona, Paris, New York. Third trip to the United States.

1962-63. Major retrospectives at Musée National d'Art Moderne in Paris, Museum of Modern Art in Tokyo (graphics), and Tate Gallery in London.

1964. Opening of the Fondation Maeght at Saint-Paul-de-Vence.

1966. Exhibition in London. Trip to Japan for major retrospective. Retrospective in Philadelphia.

1967. Receives Carnegie Prize for painting.

1968-69. Major exhibitions at Fondation Maeght, Barcelona, and Munich.

1970. Exhibition of sculptures at Galerie Maeght in Paris and in Milan. With Tápies, participates in protest against Burgos trial.

1971-73. Numerous exhibitions, many of them devoted to sculpture and *sobreteixims,* at Knokke-le-Zoute, Minneapolis, Cleveland, Chicago, Boston, London, Barcelona, Zurich, Stockholm, New York, Paris, and Saint-Paul-de-Vence.

1974. Major general retrospective and presentation of a ballet at the National Galleries in the Grand Palais.

BIBLIOGRAPHY
PRINCIPAL BOOKS ABOUT MIRÓ

L'œuvre de Joan Miró de 1917 à 1933. Special issue of *Cahiers d'Art* 1-4 (Text by R. Desnos, W. Grohmann, P. Guéguen, E. Hemingway, R. Jaffé, B. Péret, M. Raynal, H. Read, J. J. Sweeney, J. Viot, C. Zervos). Paris 1934.

Joan Miró. Special issue of *Gaceta de Arte*, No. 38 (Text by Westerdahl, R. Hoppe, V. Huidobro, L. Massine, C. Zervos). Tenerife 1936.

Sweeney, James Johnson. *Joan Miró.* Modern Art. New York 1941.

Joan Miró, Oeuvres 1944-1946, in *Cahiers d'Art,* vols. 20-21. Paris 1946.

Leiris, Michel. *Les gravures de Joan Miró.* Curt Valentin. New York 1947.

Miró. Nos. 14-15 of *Derrière le miroir.* Paris 1948.

Cirici-Pellicer, Alexandre. *Miró y la imaginacion.* Omega. Barcelona 1949.

Cirlot, Juan Eduardo. *Joan Miró.* Cobalto. Barcelona 1949.

Greenberg, Clement. *Joan Miró.* Quadrangle Press. New York 1949.

Elgar, Frank. *Miró.* Hazan. Paris 1954.

Prévert, Jacques, and Ribémont-Dessaigne, Georges. *Joan Miró.* Maeght. Paris 1956.

Verdet, André, and Hauert, Roger. *Joan Miró.* Kister. Geneva 1956.

Wember, Paul. *Miró, Das graphische Werk.* Kaiser Wilhelm Museum. Krefeld 1957.

Hüttinger, Eduard. *Miró.* Scherz, Berne, Stuttgart, Vienna 1957.

Joan Miró. Special issue of *Los Papeles de son Armadans,* T. VII, No. XXI. Madrid, Palma de Majorca 1957.

Hunter, Sam. *Joan Miró, Das graphische Werk.* Hatje. Stuttgart 1958.

Erben, Walter. *Joan Miró.* Prestel Verlag. Munich 1959.

Soby, James Thrall. *Joan Miró.* Modern Art. New York 1959.

Gomis, Joaquim, and Prats Valles, Joan. *The Miró Atmosphere.* Wittenborn, New York 1959, and Polígrafa. Barcelona 1960.

Dupin, Jacques. *Miró.* Flammarion. Paris 1961.

Weelen, Guy. *Miró.* Hazan. Paris 1961.

Gomis, Joaquim, and Prats-Valles, Joan. *Creacion Miró 1961.* Preface by Yvon Taillandier. Polígrafa. Barcelona 1962.

Perucho, Joan. *Miró-Album 19.* Sala Gaspar. Barcelona 1963.

Lassaigne, Jacques. *Miró.* Skira. Lausanne 1963.

Gasch, Sebastian. *Joan Miró.* Alcides. Barcelona 1963.

Taillandier, Yvon. *Miró. Je travaille comme un jardinier.* XXᵉ Siècle, Hazan. Paris 1964.

Gomis, Joaquim, and Prats-Valles, Joan. *Creacion en el espacio de Joan Miró.* Preface by Sir Roland Penrose. Polígrafa. Barcelona 1966.

Padrta, Jiri. *Joan Miró.* Odeon. Prague 1967.

Perucho, Juan. *Joan Miró y Cataluna.* Polígrafa. Barcelona 1968.

Bucci, Mario. *Joan Miró. Sadea-Sansoni.* Florence 1968.

Tapie, Michel. *Joan Miró.* Fratelli Fabbri. Milan 1970.

Penrose, Sir Roland. *Miró.* Thames & Hudson. London 1970.

Sweeney, J. J. *Joan Miró.* Polígrafa. Barcelona 1971.

Rowel, Margit. *Miró.* Abrams. New York 1971.

Hommage à Joan Miró. Special issue of *XXᵉ Siècle.* Paris 1972.

Dupin, Jacques. *Miró sculpteur.* Polígrafa. Barcelona 1972.

Carredor Matheos, Jose. *Miró.* Direccion de Bellas Artes. Madrid 1972.

Taillandier, Yvon. *Miró à l'encre.* XXᵉ Siècle, Paris 1972, and Gili, Barcelona 1972.

Dupin, Jacques. *Miró, der Bildhauer.* Weber. 1972.

Jouffroy, Alain, and Teixidor, Joan. *Miró, sculptures.* Maeght. Paris 1973.

Leiris, Michel. « J. M. », in *Little Review*, New York, Summer 1926, pp. 8-9.

Gasch, Sebastian. « L'obra del pintor J. M. », in *L'Amic de les Arts*, vol. I, No. 5, Sitges 1926, pp. 15-17.

Breton, André. *Le Surréalisme et la peinture*, Gallimard, Paris 1928, pp. 62-65.

George, Waldemar. « M. et le miracle ressuscité », in *Le Centauer*, No. 8, Brussels 1929, pp. 201-204.

Cahiers de Belgique. « M. », No. 2, Brussels 1929, pp. 202-215.

Einstein, Carl. « J. M. papiers collés », in *Documents*, No. 4, 1930, pp. 241-243.

Bataille, Georges. « J.M. peintures récentes », in *Documents*, No. 7, 1930, pp. 398-403.

Hugnet, Georges. « J. M. ou l'enfance de l'art », in *Cahiers d'Art*, Nos. 7-8, 1931, pp. 335-340.

Einstein, Carl. *Die Kunst des 20 Jarhunderts*, Propyläen, Berlin 1931, pp. 128, 428-433, 641.

Teriade, E. « Emancipation de la peinture », in *Minotaure*, Nos. 3-4, Dec. 1933, pp. 9-20.

Huygue, René. *Histoire de l'art contemporain*, Alcan, Paris 1935.

Soby, James T. *After Picasso*, Dodd, Mead, New York 1935.

J. M. Exhibition catalogue of the Pierre Matisse Gallery, with a list of previous exhibitions, New York 1935.

Frey, John G. « M. and the Surrealists », in *Parnassus*, vol. 8, New York 1936, pp. 13-15.

Hugnet, Georges. « A la lumière du surréalisme », in *Bulletin of the Museum of Modern Art of New York*, Nos. 2-3, Dec. 1936, pp. 19-32.

Barr, Alfred H., Jr. *Fantastic Art, Dada, Surrealism*, Museum of Modern Art, New York 1936.

Eluard, Paul. « Naissance de M. », in *Cahiers d'Art*, Nos. 1-3, 1937, pp. 78-83.

Album surréaliste, Mizué, Tokyo, June 1937.

Breton, André, and Eluard, Paul. *Dictionnaire abrégé du surréalisme*, Galerie Beaux-Arts, Paris 1938.

Zervos, Christian. *Histoire de l'Art contemporain*, Cahiers d'Art, Paris 1938.

« J. M. » in *London Bulletin*, No. 2, May 1938, pp. 3-5.

Duthuit, Georges. « Enquête », in *Cahiers d'Art*, Nos. 1-4, 1939, pp. 65-75.

Tzara, Tristan. « A propos de J. M. », in *Cahiers d'Art*, Nos. 3-4, 1940, pp. 37-47.

Watson, Peter. « J. M. », in *Horizon*, No. 20, London 1941, pp. 131-133.

Sweeney, James J. « J. M. », in *Ars*, No. 5, Mexico 1943, pp. 31-37.

Nadeau, Maurice. *Histoire du surréalisme*, Du Seuil, Paris 1945.

Gassier, Pierre. « M. et Artigas », in *Labyrinthe*, No. 22-23, Geneva 1946, pp. 10-11.

Dorival, Bernard. *Les Etapes de la peinture contemporaine*, Gallimard, Paris 1946.

Lee, Francis. « Interview with M. », in *Possibilités*, No. 1, New York 1947, pp. 66-67.

Breton, André, and Duchamp, Marcel. *Le Surréalisme en 1947*, Maeght, Paris 1947.

« M. », in *Derrière le miroir*, Nos. 14-15, Nov-Dec. 1948.

Zervos, Christian. « Remarques sur les œuvres de J. M. », in *Cahiers d'Art*, v. 24, 1949, pp. 114-138.

Gasch, Sebastia. « J. M. », in *Kunstwerk*, No. 5, Baden-Baden 1950, pp. 21-25.

Raynal, Maurice. *Histoire de la peinture moderne*, Skira, Geneva 1950.

« M. », in *Derrière le miroir*, Nos. 29-30, May-June 1950.

Duthuit, Georges. « J. M. », in *Mizué*, No. 570, Tokyo 1953, pp. 1-48.

« M. », in *Derrière le miroir*, Nos. 57-59, June 1953.

« M. », in *L'Oeil*, Nos. 7-8, 1955, pp. 52-59.

« M.-Artigas », in *Derrière le miroir*, Nos. 87-89, June 1956.

Bernier, Rosamond. « M. céramiste », in *L'Oeil*, No. 17, 1956, pp. 49-55.

Dupin, Jacques. « M. », in *Quadrum*, No. 11, Brussels 1956, pp. 95-106.

Jouffroy, Alain. « Portrait d'un artiste J. M. », in *Arts*, No. 578, July 25 1956.

Guéguen, Pierre. « L'humour féerique de J. M. », in *XXᵉ Siècle*, No. 8, 1957, pp. 39-44.

Yanaihara, I. « Les céramiques de M. », in *Mizué*, No. 620, Tokyo 1957, pp. 3-22.

Guéguen, Pierre. « J. L. Sert, l'atelier du peintre M. à Palma de Majorque », in *Aujourd'hui*, No. 15, 1957, pp. 46-49.

Breton, André. « Constellations de J. M. », in *L'Oeil*, No. 48, 1958, pp. 50-55.

Schneider, Pierre. « M. », in *Horizon*, No. 4, New York 1959, pp. 70-81.

Rubin, William. « M. in retrospect », in *Art International*, Nos. 5-6, Zurich 1959, pp. 34-41.

Jean, Marcel. *Histoire de la peinture surréaliste*, Du Seuil, Paris 1959.

Dupin, Jacques. « Vers M. », in *XXᵉ Siècle*, No. 15, 1960, pp. 102-109.

Cassou, Jean. *Panorama des arts plastiques contemporains*, Gallimard, Paris 1960.

Vallier, Dora. « Avec M. », in *Cahiers d'Art*, Nos. 33-35, 1960, pp. 160-174.

« M. céramique murale », in *Derrière le miroir*, No. 123, Feb. 1961.

Dupin, Jacques. « Nouvelles peintures de M. », in *Derrière le miroir*, Nos. 125-126, April 1961.

« M. peintures murales », in *Derrière le miroir*, No. 128, June 1961.

Chevalier, Denys. « M. », in *Aujourd'hui*, No. 39, 1962, pp. 6-13.

Volboudt, Pierre. « M. fortrollade universum », in *Konstrevy*, t. XXXVIII, Stockholm 1962, pp. 176-181.

Taillandier, Yvon. « Pour une cosmogonie de M. », in *XXᵉ Siècle*, No. 24, 1964, pp. 107-111.

Hinkel, Hans. « Arena der Imagination J. M. », in *Weltkunst*, t. XXXIV, 1964.

Perucho, Juan. « Les cartons de M. », in *XXᵉ Siècle*, t. 25, 1965, pp. 65-72.

Dupin, Jacques. « Les peintures sur carton de M. », in *Derrière le miroir*, Nos. 151-152, 1965.

Frenaud, André, Taillandier, Yvon, and Waldberg, Patrick. « M. oiseau solaire, oiseau lunaire, étincelles », in *XXᵉ Siècle*, t. 28, 1967, pp. 81-97.

Juin, Hubert. « M. », in *Arti*, No. 3, 1967, pp. 8-30.

Waldberg, Patrick. « Le miromonde », in *Derrière le miroir*, Nos. 164-165, 1967, pp. 1-25.

Warnier, Raymond. « La rétrospective M. à la Fondation Maeght », in *Colloquio*, No. 51, 1968, pp. 22-27.

Lamac, Miroslav. *Myslenky modernich maliru* (Anthology of the writings of modern painters), N.C.S. V.U., Prague 1968.

Castillo, Alberto del. « La magna exposicion J. M. en Barcelona », in *Goya*, 1968-69, pp. 294-297.

Camon Aznar, José. « El arte de M. », in *Goya* 1968-1969, pp. 286-293.

Giedion-Welcher, Carola. « J. M. und sien Werk für die moderne Kunst », in *Universitas*, t. 24, 1969, pp. 401-410.

Dupin, Jacques, and Krause, Ingrid. *J. M. Austellungsleitung*, Hans der Kunst, Munich 1969.

Castillo, Alberto del. « Cronica de Barcelona », in *Goya*, No. 90, May 1969, pp. 395-396.

Aguilera Cerni, Vincente. « M. », in *D'Ars*, Nos. 46-47, 1969, pp. 82-87.

Ashbery, J. « M. Bronze Age », in *Art News*, No. 69, May 1970, pp. 34-36.

« M. and Pierre Matisse » in *Arts*, No. 44, New York 1970.

Garcia-Herraiz, E. « Nuevos grabados de M. », in *Goya*, No. 96, May 1970.

Russel, J. « M. sculptures », in *Studio*, No. 179, May 1970, pp. 222-224.

Applegate, J. « M. », in *Art International*, No. 14, Oct. 1970.

Garcia-Herraiz, E. « M. escultura », in *Goya*, No. 99, Nov. 1970.

Ferrier, J. L. « La Vérité de M. », in *XXᵉ Siècle, No.* 35, Dec. 1970, pp. 59-67.

Balthazar, André, and Dupin, Jacques. « M. sculpteur », in *Derrière le miroir*, No. 186, 1970.

Young, J. E. « M. », in *Art International*, No. 15, April 1971.

Gilmour, P. « Four Catalan Artists », in *Connoisseur*, No. 177, May 1971.

Alechinsky, Pierre, and Dupin, Jacques. « M. peintures sur papier », in *Derrière le miroir*, Nos. 193-194, 1971.

Clay, Julien. « M. sculpteur », in *XXᵉ Siècle*, No. 33, Dec. 1971.

Schneider, Pierre. *Les dialogues du Louvre*, Denoël, Paris 1972.

M. Bronzes. The Hayward Art Gallery, London 1972.

Sylvester, David, and Dupin, Jacques. *J. M. das plastische Werk*, Kunsthaus, Zurich 1972.

J. M. Opere scelte dal 1924 al 1960. Artelevi, Milan 1972.

Bovi, A. « J. M. », in *Capitolium*, 48, No. 1, 1972, pp. 24-32.

Krauss, Rosalind, and Rovel, Margit. *M. Magnetic Fields*, Solomon R. Guggenheim Museum, New York 1973.

« M. Sobreteixims », in *Derrière le miroir*, No. 203, April 1973.

PRINCIPAL BOOKS ILLUSTRATED
BY MIRÓ

Tzara, Tristan. *L'Arbre des voyageurs.* De la Montagne. Paris 1930.

Hugnet, Georges. *Enfances.* Cahiers d'Art. Paris 1933.

Peret, Benjamin. *Au Paradis des fantômes.* Henri Parisot. Paris 1938.

Série de Barcelone. Joan Prats. Barcelona 1944.

Tzara, Tristan. *L'antitête. Bordas.* Paris 1948.

Album 13. Maeght. Paris 1948.

Tzara, Tristan. *Parler seul.* Maeght. Paris 1950.

Crevel, René. *La Bague d'aurore.* Luis Broder. Paris 1958.

Eluard, Paul. *A toute épreuve.* Gérald Cramer. Geneva 1958.

Char, René. *Nous avons.* Louis Broder. Paris 1959.

Je travaille comme un jardinier. Collected by Yvon Taillandier. XXe Siècle. Paris 1963.

Jarry, Alfred. *Ubu roi.* Tériade. Paris 1964.

Quelques Fleurs pour des amis. Text by Eugène Ionesco. XXe Siècle. Paris 1965.

Hommage à Joan Prats. Polígrafa. Barcelona 1971.

Miró, Joan. *Le Lézard aux plumes d'or.* A poem: written, designed, and illustrated. Louis Broder. Paris 1971.

Jouffroy, Alain. *Liberté des libertés.* Soleil Noir. Paris 1971.

ILLUSTRATIONS